WORLD
HISTORY SERIES ■ ■ ■

The Abolition of American Slavery

Titles in the World History Series

WORLD HISTORY SERIES

The Abolition of American Slavery

by
James Tackach

LUCENT BOOKS
SAN DIEGO, CALIFORNIA

THOMSON
™
GALE

Detroit • New York • San Diego • San Francisco
Boston • New Haven, Conn. • Waterville, Maine
London • Munich

On the cover: Harriet Tubman and the slaves she led to freedom.

Library of Congress Cataloging-in-Publication Data

Tackach, James.
    The Abolition of American Slavery / by James Tackach.
        p.   cm.—(World History Series)
    Summary: Discusses slavery in America including the in-
troduction of slaves into American society, the abolitionist
movement, the national conflict over slavery and the resulting
Civil War, emancipation, and the civil rights movement.
    Includes bibliographical references and index.
    ISBN 1-59018-002-X (hardback : alk. paper)
    1. Antislavery movements—United States—History—
Juvenile literature. 2. Slavery—United States—History—
Juvenile literature. [1. Antislavery movements. 2.
Slavery—History.] I. Title. II. Series.
E449 .T13 2002
973' .0496073—dc21

2001005301

Contents

Foreword

Each year on the first day of school, nearly every history teacher faces the task of explaining why his or her students should study history. One logical answer to this question is that exploring what happened in our past explains how the things we often take for granted—our customs, ideas, and institutions—came to be. As statesman and historian Winston Churchill put it, "Every nation or group of nations has its own tale to tell. Knowledge of the trials and struggles is necessary to all who would comprehend the problems, perils, challenges, and opportunities which confront us today." Thus, a study of history puts modern ideas and institutions in perspective. For example, though the founders of the United States were talented and creative thinkers, they clearly did not invent the concept of democracy. Instead, they adapted some democratic ideas that had originated in ancient Greece and with which the Romans, the British, and others had experimented. An exploration of these cultures, then, reveals their very real connection to us through institutions that continue to shape our daily lives.

Another reason often given for studying history is the idea that lessons exist in the past from which contemporary societies can benefit and learn. This idea, although controversial, has always been an intriguing one for historians. Those who agree that society can benefit from the past often quote philosopher George Santayana's famous statement, "Those who cannot remember the past are condemned to repeat it." Historians who subscribe to Santayana's philosophy believe that, for example, studying the events that led up to the major world wars or other significant historical events would allow society to chart a different and more favorable course in the future.

Just as difficult as convincing students of the importance of studying history is the search for useful and interesting supplementary materials that present historical events in a context that can be easily understood. The volumes in Lucent Books' World History Series attempt to present a broad, balanced, and penetrating view of the march of history. Ancient Egypt's important wars and rulers, for example, are presented against the rich and colorful backdrop of Egyptian religious, social, and cultural developments. The series engages the reader by enhancing historical events with these cultural contexts. For example, in *Ancient Greece*, the text covers the role of women in that society. Slavery is discussed in *The Roman Empire*, as well as how slaves earned their freedom. The numerous and varied aspects of everyday life in these and other societies are explored in each volume of the series. Additionally, the series covers the major political, cultural, and philosophical ideas as the torch of civilization is passed from ancient Mesopotamia and Egypt, through Greece, Rome, Medieval Europe, and other world cultures, to the modern day.

The material in the series is formatted in a thorough, precise, and organized manner. Each volume offers the reader a comprehensive and clearly written overview of an important historical event or period. The topic under discussion is placed in a broad, historical context. For example, *The Italian Renaissance* begins with a discussion of the High Middle Ages and the loss of central control that allowed certain Italian cities to develop artistically. The book ends by looking forward to the Reformation and interpreting the societal changes that grew out of the Renaissance. Thus, students are not only involved in an historical era, but also enveloped by the events leading up to that era and the events following it.

One important and unique feature in the World History Series is the primary and secondary source quotations that richly supplement each volume. These quotes are useful in a number of ways. First, they allow students access to sources they would not normally be exposed to because of the difficulty and obscurity of the original source. The quotations range from interesting anecdotes to farsighted cultural perspectives and are drawn from historical witnesses both past and present. Second, the quotes demonstrate how and where historians themselves derive their information on the past as they strive to reach a consensus on historical events. Lastly, all of the quotes are footnoted, familiarizing students with the citation process and allowing them to verify quotes and/or look up the original source if the quote piques their interest.

Finally, the books in the World History Series provide a detailed launching point for further research. Each book contains a bibliography specifically geared toward student research. A second, annotated bibliography introduces students to all the sources the author consulted when compiling the book. A chronology of important dates gives students an overview, at a glance, of the topic covered. Where applicable, a glossary of terms is included.

In short, the series is designed not only to acquaint readers with the basics of history, but also to make them aware that their lives are a part of an ongoing human saga. Perhaps then they will come to the same realization as famed historian Arnold Toynbee. In his monumental work, *A Study of History*, he wrote about becoming aware of history flowing through him in a mighty current, and of his own life "welling like a wave in the flow of this vast tide."

IMPORTANT DATES IN THE HISTORY OF THE ABOLITION OF AMERICAN SLAVERY

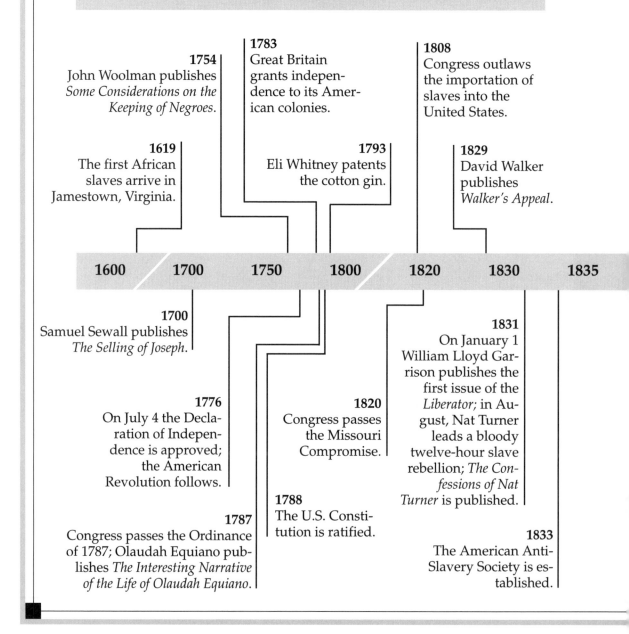

1754
John Woolman publishes *Some Considerations on the Keeping of Negroes.*

1783
Great Britain grants independence to its American colonies.

1808
Congress outlaws the importation of slaves into the United States.

1619
The first African slaves arrive in Jamestown, Virginia.

1793
Eli Whitney patents the cotton gin.

1829
David Walker publishes *Walker's Appeal.*

1600   1700   1750   1800   1820   1830   1835

1700
Samuel Sewall publishes *The Selling of Joseph.*

1776
On July 4 the Declaration of Independence is approved; the American Revolution follows.

1820
Congress passes the Missouri Compromise.

1831
On January 1 William Lloyd Garrison publishes the first issue of the *Liberator;* in August, Nat Turner leads a bloody twelve-hour slave rebellion; *The Confessions of Nat Turner* is published.

1788
The U.S. Constitution is ratified.

1787
Congress passes the Ordinance of 1787; Olaudah Equiano publishes *The Interesting Narrative of the Life of Olaudah Equiano.*

1833
The American Anti-Slavery Society is established.

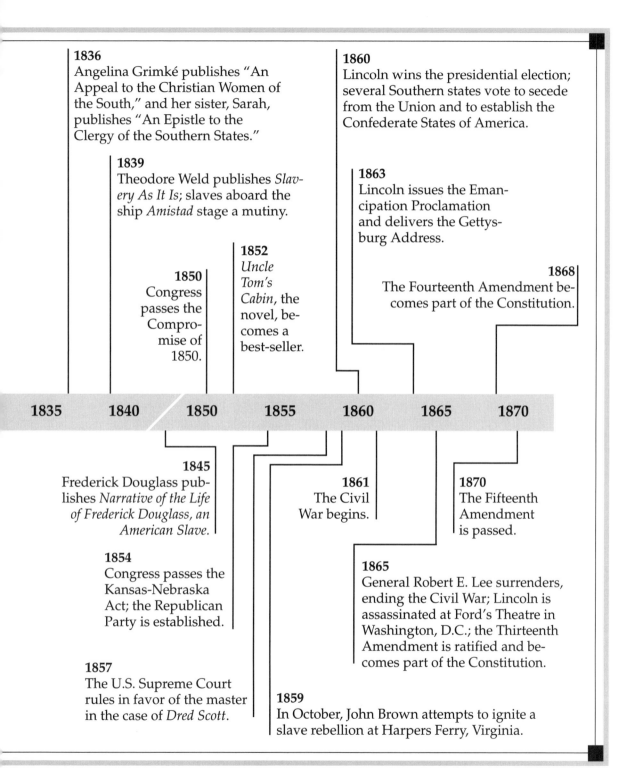

1836
Angelina Grimké publishes "An Appeal to the Christian Women of the South," and her sister, Sarah, publishes "An Epistle to the Clergy of the Southern States."

1839
Theodore Weld publishes *Slavery As It Is*; slaves aboard the ship *Amistad* stage a mutiny.

1850
Congress passes the Compromise of 1850.

1852
Uncle Tom's Cabin, the novel, becomes a best-seller.

1860
Lincoln wins the presidential election; several Southern states vote to secede from the Union and to establish the Confederate States of America.

1863
Lincoln issues the Emancipation Proclamation and delivers the Gettysburg Address.

1868
The Fourteenth Amendment becomes part of the Constitution.

1835   1840   1850   1855   1860   1865   1870

1845
Frederick Douglass publishes *Narrative of the Life of Frederick Douglass, an American Slave.*

1854
Congress passes the Kansas-Nebraska Act; the Republican Party is established.

1857
The U.S. Supreme Court rules in favor of the master in the case of *Dred Scott*.

1861
The Civil War begins.

1870
The Fifteenth Amendment is passed.

1865
General Robert E. Lee surrenders, ending the Civil War; Lincoln is assassinated at Ford's Theatre in Washington, D.C.; the Thirteenth Amendment is ratified and becomes part of the Constitution.

1859
In October, John Brown attempts to ignite a slave rebellion at Harpers Ferry, Virginia.

Slavery: America's Original Sin

Slavery took root on the continent of North America in 1619, when a group of about twenty black Africans taken from their native land by Dutch traders arrived in the British colony of Jamestown, Virginia, to be sold to settlers as farmworkers. These slaves were the first in a steady stream of Africans brought to North America against their will and sold into slavery during the seventeenth century. After 1700 a brisk slave trade developed between Africa and America. Slaves were traded for sugar, molasses, rice, and other American products and then sold at auctions in the port cities along the eastern coast of North America for distribution throughout the American colonies. During the eighteenth century more than five hundred thousand Africans were brought to North America as slaves. The U.S. Congress acted to abolish the African slave trade in 1808, but the descendants of the African slaves brought to North America during the seventeenth and eighteenth centuries became slaves at birth, and the vast majority remained slaves their entire lives.

Slavery was America's most grievous sin. The institution continued on North American soil for almost 250 years. During that period, millions of black Africans and their descendants lived and died in bondage; they labored without pay, lived under wretched conditions, were bought and sold without their consent, and often received severe punishment for any act of disobedience to their masters. Only a small percentage of American slaves were set free by their owners or managed to es-

African men are pictured in two of the earliest known photos of slaves in America.

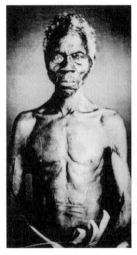

cape from bondage on their own. For most American slaves, slavery was a life-long sentence.

In 1776 the American colonies owned by Great Britain wrote the Declaration of Independence and in doing so, they established themselves as a nation dedicated to the self-evident truth "that all men are created equal; that they are endowed by their Creator with certain unalienable rights; that among these are life, liberty, and the pursuit of happiness." But the institution of slavery, a blatant contradiction of the noble sentiments articulated in America's Declaration of Independence, remained legal in some parts of the United States until 1865. The Thirteenth Amendment to the U.S. Constitution, enacted in the wake of the Civil War, ultimately outlawed slavery. Section one of that amendment stated, "Neither slavery nor involuntary servitude, except as a punishment for crime whereof the party shall have been duly convicted, shall exist within the United States, or any place subject to their jurisdiction."

OPPOSING SLAVERY

Many Americans assume that the process to abolish slavery began with the Civil War, or with the national agitation over the slavery issue that took place during the decade before that war. That notion is, to some extent, accurate. The debates over slavery between the North and the South during the 1850s split the United States in two, leading to the great civil war that commenced in 1861. During that war, President Abraham Lincoln issued the Emancipation Proclamation, which virtually assured that slavery would end on U.S. soil if the North won the war. But the process to uproot American slavery did not begin in 1861 or during the 1850s. Slavery's opponents—individuals and groups who questioned the morality of slavery and articulated the belief that slavery ought to be abolished on the American continent—surfaced soon after the first slaves came to Jamestown, Virginia. For more than two centuries, however, the voices of the abolitionists were only dimly heard; an organized, vocal American abolitionist movement did not emerge until the 1830s. Abolitionist voices sounded well before that time, however—in the Quaker meetinghouses, in the villages of Puritan New England, in the meeting rooms when America's founders crafted the words of the Declaration of Independence and the U.S. Constitution.

Ultimately, the abolitionists were successful, though it took them almost 250 years to accomplish their goal. The institution of slavery, criticized by some Americans from its inception, uprooted by the Civil War, and eventually outlawed by the Thirteenth Amendment, became a part of America's past.

1 Slavery Takes Root in America: 1619–1775

Slavery took root in North America during the seventeenth century because it was enormously profitable. Most seventeenth-century Americans made their livings on a family farm, and slaves could play a vital role in an agricultural economy. With very little training, slaves could learn to clear and plow fields, sow seed, harvest crops, tend animals, and perform other duties essential to the operation of an efficient farm. The original slaves brought to Jamestown, Virginia, in 1619—and most of the thousands who followed them to America during the seventeenth century—were sold to American farmers. Slaves could be housed, clothed, and fed cheaply enough and, in exchange, could contribute their labor to the operation of their master's farm or plantation. They would not have to be paid; they could not leave their employment for a better position or higher wages; and any children whom they would bear would become the master's property.

SLAVERY AND THE DEVELOPING AMERICAN ECONOMY

Slavery became entrenched in America as its economy developed. During the seven-teenth century most American slaves probably labored on family farms; but as the American economy became more sophisticated and diverse, slaves were trained to complete more varied tasks. Slaves living in cities became skilled craftsmen—barrel makers, blacksmiths, ship caulkers, carpenters, seamstresses, and weavers. They worked in mills and served as nurses and domestic servants. By the beginning of the eighteenth century, slavery had spread to all of Great Britain's American colonies.

During the eighteenth century a plantation economy developed in Great Britain's Southern colonies—Virginia, the Carolinas, and Georgia. Large plantations produced rice, indigo, tobacco, and other agricultural products that were shipped for export and sold in world markets. Slaves contributed the bulk of the labor on these large plantations, making the Southern plantation economy enormously profitable and creating a wealthy class of planters who owned large tracts of land. For these planters, slavery became a necessity; they could not realize such large profits if they had to employ a paid labor force to work on their plantations.

In the Northern colonies, slavery was less profitable than it was in the South. The North's growing season was much shorter—only a few months in New England—so a plantation economy like the one that emerged in the South never developed in the North. Northern slave owners would have to feed, clothe, and house slaves for the entire year but would be able to employ them productively for only a few months during the growing season. Nonetheless, slavery spread to the Northern colonies during the eighteenth century. Northern slaves performed farmwork, domestic chores like housekeeping and child rearing, and other skilled and semiskilled crafts.

American slavery developed alongside indentured servitude. During the eighteenth century, thousands of white Europeans came to America as indentured servants. They signed a contract with an American farmer or merchant to work for that person for a specified number of years in exchange for passage to America, housing, and food. When the period of indentureship ended, the indentured servant was free to move, to purchase land, and to pursue work on his or her own. Most American slaves,

Cotton plantations in the American South would have been barely profitable without the use of unpaid slave labor.

however, remained in bondage for their entire lives.

THE SLAVE TRADE

The slave trade between Africa and North America that began during the seventeenth century flourished during the eighteenth century. Black Africans on the west coast of Africa were kidnapped by international slave traders or were purchased from African tribesmen. These captured Africans were transported by ship to North America and were sold or traded in port cities such as Newport, Rhode Island; Charleston, South Carolina; Philadelphia; Boston; and New York. Thousands of slaves were also brought to the West Indies, where they labored on sugar plantations. Often the slaves were traded for rum, a colonial product sold profitably in world markets. The slaves were then sold at auctions and were transported throughout the colonies, where they were either employed or resold. Historians estimate that about twenty thousand slaves were imported to North America during the seventeenth century and close to six hundred thousand arrived during the eighteenth century.

Many slave traders became wealthy international businessmen. Most slave traders were British or Dutch; but during the eighteenth century when the slave trade became extremely profitable, an increasing number of entrepreneurial Americans became engaged in slave trading.

Often slave traders shipped and traded other products as well. A slave trader might transport slaves from Africa to America, trade them for rum in an American port city like Newport, Rhode Island, then transport the rum to Great Britain for sale there.

THE MIDDLE PASSAGE

African slaves were transported to America in wretched conditions. Scores of slaves were packed tightly in the bowels of sailing vessels; often the slaves were bound or shackled during the entire trip, which could take several weeks. The slaves were poorly fed, drinking water was minimal, and conditions aboard the ship were often grossly unsanitary. The slave's arduous journey from Africa to America became known as the Middle Passage.

Olaudah Equiano, born in Africa around 1745, was kidnapped into slavery when he was about eleven years old. In 1789, more than twenty years after he had gained his freedom, Equiano published a narrative of his life in bondage titled *The Interesting Narrative of the Life of Olaudah Equiano, or Gustavus Vassa, the African*. In that text, which was originally published in London, Equiano described the shameful conditions aboard the ship that transported him to America. "The stench of the hold . . . was so intolerably loathsome, that it was dangerous to remain there for any time," stated Equiano. "This deplorable situation was again aggravated by the galling of the chains . . .

and the filth of the necessary tubs [for human waste], into which the children often fell, and were almost suffocated."[1] Historians claim that the casualty rate aboard the worst slave ships approached 50 percent. Slaves died of disease, starvation, and even suicide.

EARLY ABOLITIONIST VOICES

Although slavery spread rapidly across America during the seventeenth and eighteenth centuries, the institution did not take root without opposition. Historians claim that some settlers in Jamestown, Virginia, objected to slavery when it was

African slaves were packed into the lower decks of slave ships like boxes of cargo. As many as 50 percent of them died of disease, starvation, and suicide.

introduced there in 1619. But these early abolitionists either did not record their opposition to slavery in writing, or their writings have not survived.

During the 1680s British Quakers began immigrating to America to settle in Pennsylvania with their leader, William Penn. Penn had founded the Pennsylvania colony as a so-called holy experiment committed to religious and political freedom and democratic government. Most of these original Quaker settlers were vehemently antislavery, condemning the institution on political, moral, and religious grounds; their descendants would remain staunchly abolitionist until American slavery was abolished. But the Quakers' opposition to slavery did little to stop its spread during the late seventeenth and eighteenth centuries. According to literary historian Mason Lowance, "The Quakers, who had opposed slavery in Great Britain, developed arguments against the expansion of chattel slavery in North America, but their voices were muted compared to the overwhelming economic development of the plantation system in the Southern colonies."[2] Although many Quakers were opposed to slavery, some purchased slaves to work on their farms, and the Quakers did not formally prohibit members of their faith from owning slaves until the 1770s.

THE OLDEST SURVIVING ABOLITIONIST TEXT

The earliest abolitionist document that has survived was written by a Puritan magistrate in colonial Boston in 1700. Samuel Sewall was born in Great Britain in 1652 and was brought to America by his Puritan parents when he was a child. As a young man he attended Harvard College; when his studies were completed, he embarked on a successful career in business and politics. In 1700 Sewall sat as a judge of the Massachusetts Superior Court. His duties from the bench drew him into a debate with another judge, John Saffin, on the morality and legality of slavery. In one case Saffin had ruled that a black indentured servant could not be set free when his term of indentureship expired, even though that term had been set down in a written contract. In response, Sewall composed a document titled *The Selling of Joseph, a Memorial*.

Sewall based his opposition to slavery on the Bible. In *The Selling of Joseph*, he asserted that "all Men, as they are the Sons of *Adam*, are Coheirs; and have equal Right unto Liberty, and all their outward Comforts of Life." Sewall referred to the Old Testament story of Joseph, who was sold into slavery in Egypt by his brothers: "*Joseph* was rightfully no more a Slave to his Brethren, than they were to him; and they had no more Authority to *Sell* him, than they had to *Slay* him." Sewall argued that men had no right to separate what God has joined together—"Men from their Country, Husbands from their Wives, Parents from their Children." Sewall also noted the immorality of the gruesome Middle Passage that brought slaves from Africa to America: "How horrible is the Uncleanness, Mortality, if not Murder, that the ships

THE MIDDLE PASSAGE

In a speech to a grand jury in Maine in 1820, Joseph Story, an attorney, described the crowded conditions aboard slave ships as they made their journey from Africa to America. His description is excerpted from editor Mason Lowance's Against Slavery: An Abolitionist Reader.

"When the number of slaves is completed, the ships begin what is called the middle passage, to transport the slaves to the colonies.—The height of the apartments in the ships is different according to the size of the vessel, and it is from six feet to three feet, so that it is impossible to stand erect in most of the vessels, and in some scarcely to sit down in the same posture. In the best regulated ships, a grown person is allowed but sixteen inches in width, thirty-two inches in height, and five feet eleven inches in length, or to use the expressive language of a witness, not so much room as a man has in his coffin.— They are indeed so crowded below that it is almost impossible to walk through the groups without treading on some of them; and if they are reluctant to get into their places they are compelled by the lash of a whip."

A slave trader walks through a slave ship.

JOHN SAFFIN'S REPLY TO *THE SELLING OF JOSEPH*

In 1700 John Saffin sat as a judge on the Massachusetts Superior Court with Samuel Sewall, the author of the antislavery tract, The Selling of Joseph. *In 1701 he composed a response to Sewall's document, and in doing so he expressed the racial views of many white American colonists. His reply is found in* Against Slavery: An Abolitionist Reader, *edited by Mason Lowance.*

"That Honourable and Learned Gentleman, the Author of a Sheet, Entitled, *The Selling of Joseph, A Memorial,* seems from thence to draw this conclusion, that because the Sons of *Jacob* did very ill in selling their Brother *Joseph* to the *Ishmaelites,* who were Heathens, therefore it is utterly unlawful to Buy and Sell Negroes, though among Christians; which conclusion I presume is not well drawn from the Premises, nor is the case parallel; for it was unlawful for the *Israelites* to sell their Brethren upon any account, or pretense whatsoever during life. But it was not unlawful for the Seed of *Abraham* to have Bond men, and Bond women either born in their House, or bought with their Money. . . .

So God hath set different Orders and Degrees of Men in the World, both in Church and Common weal. Now if this position of parity [between the races] should be true [as Sewall suggests], it would then follow that the ordinary Course of Divine Providence of God in the World should be wrong, and unjust (which we must not dare to think, much less to affirm) and all the sacred Rules, Precepts and Commands of the Almighty . . . would be of no purpose."

are guilty of that bring great Crouds of the miserable men, and Women."[3]

Sewall's document was printed as a pamphlet and was distributed throughout the Massachusetts Bay Colony. Although slavery existed in Massachusetts—Reverend Samuel Parris, a key figure in the Salem Witch Trials of 1692 owned a slave from Barbados named Tituba—

many of the Puritans who settled in New England opposed slavery on religious grounds. Cotton Mather, the renowned Puritan clergyman whose family owned slaves, spoke for many Puritans when he wrote, in 1706, *"Who can tell that this Poor Creature may belong to the Election of God!"*[4] Mather was speculating that slaves, though occupying a lowly station in life, might be destined for eternal salvation.

OTHER ABOLITIONIST VOICES

Samuel Sewall's *The Selling of Joseph* was not the only antislavery tract published during the first half of the eighteenth century. In 1739 a group of antislavery citizens from Darien, Georgia, published an appeal to Governor James Ogelthorpe to make slavery illegal in that colony. Their petition stated, "It's shocking to human Nature, that any Race of Mankind, and their Posterity, should be sentenced to perpetual Slavery; . . . and as Freedom to them must be as dear as to us, what a Scene of Horror must it bring about!"[5]

In 1754 John Woolman, a Quaker minister, authored an antislavery text titled *Some Consideration on the Keeping of Negroes*. Like Sewall's, Woolman's opposition to slavery was, for the most part, religiously based. According to Woolman, for one people to enslave another is immoral, as "God's Love is universal." Woolman also asserted the essential equality of all human beings, regardless of race or color: "The Colour of a Man avails nothing, in Matters of Right and Equity." In Woolman's view, "*Negroes* are our Fellow Creatures, and their present Condition amongst us requires our serious Consideration."[6]

At one point in his life, Woolman worked for an attorney as a scrivener, a person who made copies of deeds, contracts, and other legal documents. Once Woolman's duties called for him to copy a purchase agreement for the sale of a slave. Woolman performed his duty reluctantly, but he vowed never again to connect himself with any activity involving slaves. In his journal, which was published in book form after his death, Woolman recorded an episode involving a man who asked him to compose a will for his dying brother. The dying man expressed his desire to leave his slaves to his children. Hearing about the slaves, Woolman refused to write the will: "I told the man that I believed the practice of continuing slavery . . . was not right and had a scruple in mind against doing any writings of that kind: that though many in our Society kept them as slaves, still I was not easy to be concerned in it and desired to be excused from going to write the will."[7]

ISOLATED ABOLITIONIST VOICES

The antislavery voices of Sewall and Woolman were isolated and dimly heard in colonial America. Slavery expanded throughout the American colonies. Slaves continued to pour into America on slave ships, and the descendants of these black Africans became slaves at birth and remained in bondage throughout their lifetimes. Slavery became an important component of the colonial economy; its elimination from American soil would have caused severe economic consequences. Moreover, many colonial Americans came to assume that slaves, whose skin color, language, and culture were so different from those of the typical European, were inferior human beings whose proper place in society was to serve white people.

Some colonial Americans found the institution of slavery distasteful, but no organized abolitionist movement formed in colonial America. The abolitionist position would be embraced by an increasing number of Americans after the American Revolution, but a vocal and organized abolitionist movement would not form on American soil until the nineteenth century.

Chapter

2 Slavery in the Early American Republic: 1776–1830

The relationship between Great Britain and its American colonies deteriorated during the 1770s as the colonies and the mother country fell into dispute over taxation, self-government, and other political issues. Those disagreements led, in 1775, to armed conflict between colonial citizens and British troops. In 1776 the Second Continental Congress convened in Philadelphia to form a plan to deal with the escalating crisis that had developed between the colonies and Great Britain. On July 4 the Continental Congress voted unanimously to declare the British colonies free and independent states. The American Revolution followed the call for independence; and in 1783, after seven years of war, Great Britain granted the colonies their independence.

The American Revolution afforded the American colonies the opportunity to establish a new nation with a new form of government based on new principles. Slavery was an institution begun when the American colonies belonged to Great Britain, and it could be cast out when Great Britain surrendered its claim on the thirteen American colonies. Some of America's revolutionary leaders called for slavery's removal from American soil.

However, the opportunity to abolish slavery after the American Revolution passed, and slavery became a part of the early American republic.

SLAVERY AND THE DECLARATION OF INDEPENDENCE

When the Second Continental Congress voted to declare the colonies' independence from Great Britain, it called on Thomas Jefferson, a Virginia representative, to write the formal Declaration of Independence. Jefferson's document boldly asserted the fundamental equality of all men:

> We hold these truths to be self-evident, that all men are created equal, that they are endowed by their Creator with certain unalienable Rights, that among these are Life, Liberty, and the pursuit of Happiness. That to secure these rights, Governments are instituted among Men, deriving their just powers from the consent of the governed.

In Jefferson's view, man's right to life, liberty, and the pursuit of happiness was God-given, and it was the duty of government to protect those rights for its citizens.

In his original draft of the Declaration of Independence, Thomas Jefferson included his misgivings about the institution of slavery; however, the Continental Congress deleted those clauses from the final document.

After asserting those noble principles, Jefferson's document went on to list specific accusations against King George III of England. The king had dissolved the colonial legislative bodies; he had levied taxes against the colonies without their consent; he had kept standing armies among the citizenry during peacetime; he had denied colonial citizens accused of crimes the benefits of trial by jury. To this list, Jefferson added the charge that King George had "waged cruel war against human nature itself, violating its most sacred right of life and liberty in the persons of a distant peo-ple who never offended him, captivating them into slavery in another hemisphere, or to incur miserable death in their transportation thither."[8] Although Jefferson had been raised in a slave-owning family of Virginia planters, he had grave misgivings about the institution of slavery; he wished to express his unease about slavery in his new nation's founding document.

When Jefferson presented his Declaration of Independence to the entire Continental Congress, however, the delegates from the Southern colonies objected to his statements about slavery. These delegates represented Southern planters whose fortunes depended greatly on slave labor. To gain unanimous support for Jefferson's Declaration of Independence, the Continental Congress struck from the document the clauses concerning slavery. Hence, an opportunity was lost to tie the abolition of slavery to the American colonies' struggle for independence. The war that followed the issuance of the declaration resulted in independence for the American colonies, but American slaves remained in bondage. Ironically, the man who authored the Declaration of Independence held slaves throughout his lifetime; and after his wife's death, Jefferson fathered slave children with one of his slaves, Sally Hemmings.

SLAVERY AND THE PHILADELPHIA CONVENTION OF 1787

After achieving their independence from Great Britain, the self-governing American states operated for four years

A NEW JERSEY QUAKER CONDEMNS SLAVERY

In 1783 David Cooper, a New Jersey Quaker, distributed A Serious Address *to the members of the New Jersey State Assembly. In that document, Cooper highlights the contradiction between Americans' demand for their political rights and their denial of those rights to slaves. The following is excerpted from* Slavery: Opposing Viewpoints *by editor William Dudley.*

"However habit and custom may have rendered familiar the degrading and ignominious distinctions, which are made between people with a black skin and ourselves, I am not ashamed to declare myself an advocate for the rights of that highly injured and abused people; and were I master of . . . resistless persuasion . . . could not employ it better, than in vindicating their rights as men, and forcing a blush on every American slaveholder, who has complained of the treatment we have received from Britain; which is no more to be equaled, with ours to Negroes, than a barley corn is to the globe we inhabit. Must not every generous foreigner feel a secret indignation rise in his breast, when he hears the language of Americans upon any of their own rights as freemen being in the least infringed, and reflects that these very people are holding thousands and tens of thousands of their innocent fellow men in the most debasing and abject slavery, deprived of every right of freemen, except light and air? How similar to an atrocious pirate, setting in all the solemn pomp of a judge, passing sentence of death on a petty thief."

under the Articles of Confederation, a constitution enacted in 1781, during the American Revolution. The articles bound the former British colonies into a confederation of independent states that would unite for common defense and work together to promote trade, coin money, manage a postal service, and arrange treaties with other nations. That arrangement led to some disagreements between states and to other political problems after the Revolutionary War; thus, in 1787 delegates from each state met in Philadelphia to amend the Articles of Confederation. However, the delegates at the Philadelphia Convention of 1787 scrapped the Articles of Confederation and proposed the creation of a new republic, the United States of America. The new nation would be held together by a constitution initially comprising seven articles and ten amendments, known as the Bill of Rights.

Slavery was not a specific issue of discussion at the Philadelphia Convention. No delegate proposed the elimination of slavery or limitations on slavery in the new republic, though at one point in the convention George Mason, a delegate from Virginia, condemned the presence of slaves in the new nation. "Every master of slaves is born a petty tyrant; they bring the judgment of heaven on a country," he declared. But delegates to the convention from the South argued that slavery was vital to their region's economy; it could not be abolished. "South Carolina and Georgia cannot do without slaves,"[9] asserted Charles Cotesworth Pinckney, a Carolin-

ian. No formal motion either to abolish or restrict slavery was put forward at the Philadelphia Convention, though the convention delegates agreed that the importation of slaves into the United States would end in 1808.

Slavery and the U.S. Constitution

The new U.S. Constitution, which received approval from the states in 1788 and went into effect the following year, did not mention the words slave or slavery, but the document, in two articles, alluded to slavery, thereby giving the institution legal recognition. In section 2 of article 1, the Constitution addressed the issue of representation in the House of Representatives. A state's population dictates the number of representatives that the state can send to the House, and the representatives of the Southern states at the Philadelphia Convention wished to have slaves included in the population count. Some convention delegates from the North objected because slaves were not considered citizens. A compromise, known as the three-fifths compromise, was struck, allowing "the whole number of free persons . . . [and] three-fifths of all other persons" to be counted to determine a state's representation in the House. In other words, five slaves would be counted as three residents to determine House representation.

Slavery is also alluded to in section 2 of article 4, which states, "No person held to service or labor in one State, under the laws thereof, escaping into another, shall, in consequence of any law or regulation therein,

$100 REWARD!

RANAWAY

From the undersigned, living on Current River, about twelve miles above Doniphan, in Ripley County, Mo., on 2nd of March, 1860, **A NE GRO MAN,** about 30 years old, weighs about 160 pounds; high forehead, with a scar on it; had on brown pants and coat very much worn, and an old black wool hat; shoes size No. 11.

The above reward will be given to any person who may apprehend this said negro out of the State; and fifty dollars if apprehended in this State outside of Ripley county, or $25 if taken in Ripley county.

APOS TUCKER.

The U.S. Constitution recognized slaves as property owned and controlled by their masters. As a result, slaveholders offered rewards for the return of their runaway slaves.

be discharged from such service or labor, but shall be delivered up on claim of the party to whom such service or labor may be due." This clause referred specifically to runaway slaves, essentially mandating that escaped slaves must be returned to their owners. Hence, the Constitution recognized the status of slaves as property owned and controlled by their masters.

THE NORTHERN STATES ABOLISH SLAVERY

Even though the Constitution recognized the legality of slavery, the Northern states began to act on their own to abolish it within their own jurisdictions. Some states had initiated that step even before the American colonies achieved independence from Great Britain. As the North's economy became less focused on agriculture and more focused on manu-

facturing, the need for a slave workforce diminished. For the North's small farmers, craftsmen, and merchants, slavery became economically unviable. Moreover, many Northern political and business leaders—Benjamin Franklin, for example, who considered slavery "an atrocious debasement of human nature"[10]—expressed the view that slavery was immoral and ought to be abolished, and that the institution was incompatible with the principles articulated in the Declaration of Independence.

Between 1774 and 1804 all of the states north of the Mason-Dixon Line abolished slavery. Some states passed immediate emancipation laws; other states passed laws that would gradually abolish slavery over a period of time. For example, in 1774 the Rhode Island General Assembly passed a bill prohibiting the importation of slaves into the colony. That same assembly later decreed that

BEN FRANKLIN'S OPPOSITION TO SLAVERY

Benjamin Franklin was an active member of the Pennsylvania Society for Promoting the Abolition of Slavery. In 1789 he penned "An Address to the Public" from that society advocating the abolition of slavery because the institution debased human beings. This address is excerpted from editor Emory Elliott's American Literature: A Prentice Hall Anthology.

"Slavery is such an atrocious debasement of human nature, that its very extirpation [extermination], if not performed with solicitous [extreme] care, may sometimes open a source of serious evils.

The unhappy man, who has long been treated as a brute animal, too frequently sinks beneath the common standard of the human species. The galling chains that bind his body, do also fetter his intellectual faculties, and impair the social affections of his heart. Accustomed to move like a mere machine, by the will of a master, reflection is suspended; he has not the power of choice; and reasons and conscience have but little influence over his conduct, because he is chiefly governed by the passion of fear. He is poor and friendless; perhaps worn out by extreme labor, age, and disease."

no Rhode Islander could be born into slavery; thus, slavery would end in Rhode Island when the existing slaves passed on. In 1799 New York passed a law mandating that New Yorkers born into slavery after July 4 of that year must be set free at age twenty-eight (for men) and twenty-five (for women). This law ensured that New York would be slave-free after 1827.

While slavery was gradually dying out in the North, however, it was becoming more vital to the South's agricultural economy. At the start of the nineteenth century, slavery rapidly expanded in the Southern states because of the invention, in 1793, of a machine called the cotton gin.

COTTON BECOMES KING

In 1793 Eli Whitney, a Massachusetts farmer's son and a Yale University graduate, secured a patent for a machine that quickly removed seeds from freshly picked cotton balls. The time-consuming process of removing the seed from the cotton fiber had previously been done by hand. After the invention of Whitney's cotton gin, which could be easily duplicated by even an untrained mechanic, cotton became an extremely profitable crop in the South. The South's soil and climate were perfect for the growing of cotton. The laborious tasks of tending the cotton and picking the fiber from the plant could be performed by slaves with very little training. In addition, cotton was a cash crop. It could be shipped to the North or exported to Great Britain and turned into cloth in textile mills.

In the early nineteenth century, cotton plantations spread across the South. Land was cheap, and ambitious Southern planters could raise an extensive cotton crop that could be quickly turned into cash. The money could be used to purchase additional slaves at slave auctions, and those slaves would, in turn, allow a planter to produce even more cotton. When cotton developed into the South's major crop at the turn of the nineteenth century, slavery became even more deeply embedded in the South's economy. Slavery's proponents argued that abolishing slavery would be economically impossible. Southern planters defended the institution with great fervor; their wealth and the South's entire economy came to depend on slavery.

The invention of the cotton gin made it easier and even more profitable to raise cotton using slave labor.

Slavery Defended

As slavery became more vital to the South's plantation economy, most Southerners defended the institution on moral and religious grounds as well. In the early nineteenth century, many white Americans believed that black people were naturally inferior to whites. They viewed black skin as unattractive and as a badge of inferiority. Many whites also found black people's customs, language, and religion alien and exotic and, therefore, inferior to white European culture. In the view of many whites, the proper role for the black race to play in human affairs was to serve white people. Whites, in turn, were to provide blacks with the material comforts that they needed to survive. Slavery's proponents argued that Southern slavery established the proper relationship between the white and black races. Blacks served their white masters with their labor; in return, the master provided food, shelter, and clothing for his slaves.

Many Southern clergymen defended slavery. They maintained that slaves were the descendants of Ham of the Old Testament book of Genesis. Ham was a son of Noah who offended his father and was condemned, with all of his descendants, to be a servant of servants. Many Southern clergymen preached that God, by allowing children to be born into slavery, was justifying the institution. The South's religious leaders argued that slaves had no right to object to their positions because God, by creating them as slaves, had deemed that they were put on the earth to serve their white masters.

Not all Southerners defended the morality of slavery. Thomas Jefferson and George Washington, both Virginia slave owners whose plantations depended heavily on slave labor, acknowledged slavery's integral role in the South's economy, but questioned the morality of slavery and expressed their belief that the institution was potentially harmful to their nation. In his *Notes on the State of Virginia*, published in 1785, Jefferson stated, "The whole commerce between master and slave is a perpetual exercise of the

Slavery's proponents believed that the proper role for the black race was to serve white people.

A Defense of Slavery

In 1773 the graduation ceremony at Harvard University featured a debate on slavery. Theodore Parsons, the son of a slaveholding minister, defended slavery and bolstered his position by offering the popular argument that American slaves were better off than free Africans. His argument is found in editor William Dudley's Slavery: Opposing Viewpoints.

"Figure to yourself my friend, you are not unacquainted with *African* history, figure to yourself the delightful situation of a natural inhabitant of *Africa*. View him necessarily destitute of every mean of improvement in social virtue, of every advantage for the cultivation of those principles of humanity, in which alone consists the dignity of the rational nature, and from which only source spring all that pleasure, that happiness of life, by which the human species is distinguished from the other parts of the animal creation. Consider his situation as a candidate for an eternal existence; view him as necessarily ignorant of every principle of that religion, through the happy influence of which alone the degenerate race of Adam can rationally form the more distant expectation of future felicity.... Behold him actually clothed in all that brutal stupidity, that savage barbarity which naturally springs from such a source. Add to this, his condition of perpetual insecurity, arising from the state of hostility and war that forever rages in those inhospitable climes [climates]."

most boisterous passions, the most unremitting despotism on the one part, and degrading submissions on the other." Jefferson worried that God would eventually punish America for the sin of slavery: "Indeed I tremble for my country when I reflect that God is just; that his justice cannot sleep forever."[11] When he became president, Washington stated that it was "among my first wishes to see some plan adopted by the Legislature by which slavery in this Country may be abolished by slow, sure, and imperceptible degrees."[12] But both Jefferson and Washington died before their wish to abolish slavery in the United States became a reality.

Actions Against Slavery

While slavery was becoming entrenched in the South, some actions were taking place to restrict or eliminate the institution. In 1787 the thirteen states, still operating under the Articles of Confederation, passed the Ordinance of 1787, which stipulated that slavery would be illegal in U.S. territory north and west of the Ohio

River. During the 1790s a series of slave revolts in the French-owned island of Saint Domingue (now Haiti) in the West Indies resulted in the abolition of slavery there and the end of French rule. In 1808 the importation of slaves into the United States became illegal. The ban on importation virtually ended the Africa-to-America slave trade, though slaves were still smuggled illegally into the United States until the Civil War. Moreover, slaves could still be legally traded within the United States. As a result, slave families could potentially be broken apart at the auction block.

But the outlawing of the slave trade actually did little to curtail the expansion of slavery throughout the South. U.S. census records show that the nation contained nearly 1.2 million slaves in 1810, two years after the ban on slave importation took effect. In 1820 more than 1.5 million slaves were living in the United States, and that total increased to more than 2 million in 1830 and to almost 2.5 million in 1840. The South had no need to import slaves; the slave population increased naturally because the descendants of slaves became slaves at birth.

AN ERA OF GOOD FEELING

As the nineteenth century began, the slave-free North and the slaveholding South reached a stable compromise on the issue of slavery. It would remain legal in the South, where it was vital to the region's economy,

A black family is sold at a slave auction in Richmond, Virginia.

and it would be illegal in the North. Under that agreement, both regions prospered economically. The North became more industrialized as mills and factories were developed, and the South remained agrarian. The new nation also achieved political stability; the experiment of democratic government set down in the Constitution seemed to be working. The nation experienced no major political uprisings when one political party was voted out of office or when a president's term ended and a new president moved into the White House. A two-year war with Great Britain—the War of 1812—threatened the existence of the new nation, but that conflict ended with a peace treaty that resolved the major causes of the war.

A period of peace, political stability, and economic prosperity followed the War of 1812, a period that historians sometimes call the Era of Good Feeling. The nation expanded and pioneers moved westward to settle in Kentucky, Illinois, and Missouri. But the slavery issue would not disappear. It came to the top of the nation's political agenda in 1819, when the territory of Missouri applied for statehood.

THE DEBATE OVER MISSOURI

By 1804 the original thirteen states had settled the issue of slavery within their own borders. As new states came into the United States, however, Congress faced the decision of whether slavery would be legal or illegal in each state. Since the Ordinance of 1787 outlawed slavery in U.S. territory north and west of the Ohio River,

the states carved out of that territory— Ohio, Indiana, and Illinois—became free states when they came into the Union. Slavery was deemed legal in territories south of the Ohio River, and those territories became the slave states of Kentucky, Tennessee, Mississippi, and Alabama.

In 1803, during the Jefferson presidency, the United States purchased from France a large tract of land west of the Mississippi River known as the Louisiana Territory. By 1815 thousands of pioneers were crossing the Mississippi River and settling in the region that became known as Missouri. In 1819 the residents of Missouri applied for admission to the Union as a state. Congress had to consider the question of whether Missouri would be admitted to the Union as a slave or a free state. Missouri already held some slaves, however, as settlers from Kentucky and Tennessee had come to Missouri with their human property.

The congressional deliberation over Missouri's admission to the Union turned into an angry debate over slavery. Representative Eugene Tallmadge of New York proposed an amendment to the bill for Missouri statehood that would make the importation of slaves to Missouri illegal and would free the children of slaves already living in Missouri at the age of twenty-five. Representatives from the Southern states strenuously objected to the Tallmadge Amendment, which would eventually make Missouri a free state; they wanted Missouri admitted to the Union as a slave state.

When Missouri applied for statehood, the Union comprised twenty-two states— eleven free states and eleven slave states.

Southerners surmised that at least five Northern territories would apply for statehood in the next two decades, but only two Southern territories would likely enter the Union during the same period. Southerners wanted Missouri admitted as a slave state so that the free states would not outnumber the slave states in the U.S. Senate, where each state, regardless of population, seated two delegates. The Tallmadge Amendment received approval in the House of Representatives, where the free states held a majority, but the bill was blocked in the Senate by Southern proslavery senators. Hence, Congress continued to debate the question of slavery in Missouri.

THE MISSOURI COMPROMISE

When the Tallmadge Amendment failed, Senator J. B. Thomas of Illinois proposed a compromise. Missouri would be admitted to the United States as a slave state at the same time that Maine, a territory belonging to Massachusetts that was ready for statehood, would enter the Union as a free state, preserving the balance between free and slave states. In addition, slavery would be outlawed in portions of the Louisiana Territory north of the latitude mark of 36°30'. This plan, known as the Missouri Compromise or the Compromise of 1820, received approval by both houses of Congress and was signed into law by President James Madison in March 1820.

The Missouri Compromise, for a time, seemed to settle the question of slavery in America. But this issue would not completely go away. Thomas Jefferson, in retirement from politics at his Virginia estate, saw in the bitter debate over Missouri's statehood potential problems in the future between the North and the South; he sensed that the nation would one day be hopelessly divided over the issue of slavery. Writing to his friend John Holmes in 1820, Jefferson stated, "A geographical line, coinciding with a marked principle, moral and political, once conceived and held up to the angry passions of men, will never be obliterated; and every new irritation will mark it deeper and deeper."[13]

Another American, David Walker, a free African American, made an even more calamitous prediction in 1829 in his antislavery pamphlet titled *Walker's Appeal in Four Acts*:

> There are not a more wretched, ignorant, miserable and abject set of beings in the world than the blacks in the southern and western sections of this country, under tyrants and devils. . . . O Americans! Americans! I call God—I call angels—I call men, to witness, that your *destruction* is at hand, and will be speedily consummated unless you *repent*.[14]

For Walker, repentance involved immediately purging the nation of slavery. During the next decade, the 1830s, other strong abolitionist voices would reiterate Walker's appeal and launch an organized movement to abolish slavery in the United States.

Chapter

3 The Beginnings of the Abolitionist Movement: 1831–1849

David Walker died from mysterious causes in 1830, a year after his antislavery pamphlet, *Walker's Appeal,* was published. The abolitionist cause did not die with Walker, however; it was taken up the following year by William Lloyd Garrison, a twenty-five-year-old Massachusetts editor. On January 1, 1831, Garrison published the first issue of the *Liberator,* an antislavery newspaper that soon enjoyed a large circulation among New England abolitionists. With Garrison as their leader, the New England abolitionists would launch an antislavery movement that would spread across the United States. A handful of other important abolitionist newspapers were soon in circulation, bringing the issue of slavery to the front pages of the nation's newspapers. During the 1830s and 1840s, slavery would become the single most important, and most divisive, political issue in the nation; and by the 1850s, the United States would be hopelessly divided over slavery.

A CHILD OF POVERTY

Garrison was born in Newburyport, Massachusetts, in 1805 and was raised in

poverty. His father deserted the family when Garrison was a child, and his mother worked as a domestic servant to support her children. Having little formal education, Garrison essentially taught himself to read and, as a teenager, became a printer's apprentice. At age twenty-one he purchased a newspaper, the *Essex*

William Lloyd Garrison, along with other New England abolitionists, launched an antislavery movement that spread across the United States.

Courant, and renamed it the *Newburyport Free Press.* That paper launched Garrison's remarkable editorial career.

Garrison had developed an early disliking for slavery, perhaps because he saw his mother work under conditions that were only marginally better than those of a slave. Early in his newspaper career he became acquainted with Benjamin Lundy, another Massachusetts abolitionist, and together they edited the *Genius of Universal Emancipation,* one of the nation's first abolitionist newspapers. In 1829, the same year that Walker published his *Appeal,* Garrison addressed the American Colonization Society—an organization devoted to sending freed slaves to a colony in Africa—on the evils of slavery. In that fiery address, Garrison called slavery "a gangrene preying upon our vitals—an earthquake rumbling under our feet—a mine accumulating materials for a national catastrophe."[15] He was predicting that slavery would one day cause a calamity that would ruin the United States.

In the first issue of the *Liberator,* Garrison warned slaveholders that if slavery were not soon abolished in the United States, the slaves would violently rebel against their masters and bathe the South in blood. The main editorial in the first issue of the *Liberator* clearly and boldly asserted Garrison's purpose: "I shall strenuously contend for the immediate enfranchisement of our slave population. . . . I am in earnest—I will not equivocate—I will not excuse—I will not retreat a single inch—AND I WILL BE HEARD."[16] With the publication of the *Liberator,* Garrison became the unofficial leader of the New England abolitionist movement. So vehement was Garrison's antislavery rhetoric that several months after he began to publish the *Liberator,* the Georgia legislature declared him a criminal and offered a reward of five thousand dollars for his arrest.

Nat Turner's Rebellion

Garrison and his newspaper were blamed for a slave rebellion that occurred in the summer of 1831, an event that startled the entire nation. On August 22, just after midnight, Nat Turner, a slave living in Southampton County, Virginia, led a twelve-hour slave rebellion that took the lives of sixty white people, including children. Before dawn on that day, Turner, a self-ordained minister who claimed to have received commands from God to strike at slaveholders, moved from house to house with his followers executing slaveholding families. Later, Turner vividly described some of his grisly work: "Miss Margaret, when I discovered her, had concealed herself in the corner, formed by the projection of the cellar cap from the house; on my approach she fled, but soon was overtaken, and after repeated fatal blows with a sword, I killed her by a blow on the head, with a fence rail."[17] Turner and his followers committed similar acts in several other Southampton households.

But Nat Turner's rebellion was quickly suppressed. The day after the insurrection began, Turner's band of rebels scattered after encounters with local slaveholders

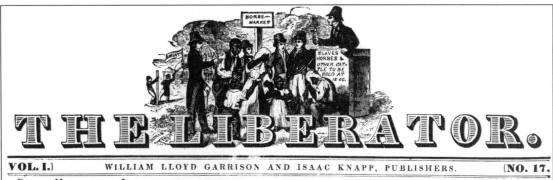

With the help of the Liberator, *the debate over slavery became the most important political issue of the day.*

and militia. Many of Turner's followers were captured, quickly tried, and executed. Turner remained at large until October 30, when he was apprehended. He was tried and convicted on November 5 and was hanged six days later. Before his execution, however, Turner narrated to an attorney, Thomas Gray, the story of his rebellion. Two weeks after Turner's death, Gray published *The Confessions of Nat Turner*, a vivid account of the Southampton slave insurrection. In this text, Turner explained the motives that prompted his rebellion, presenting his claim that he had been urged by the Holy Ghost to strike against the slaveholders:

I heard a loud noise in the heavens, and the Spirit instantly appeared to me and said the Serpent was loosened, and Christ had laid down the yoke he had borne for the sins of men, and that I should take it on and fight against the Serpent, for the time was fast approaching when the first should be last and the last should be first.[18]

The Confessions of Nat Turner shocked the nation. Proslavery Americans—many of whom blamed Garrison for inciting Turner's rebellion—saw Turner as an agent of Satan set loose from hell to do the devil's work. Abolitionists like Garrison

THE

CONFESSIONS

OF

NAT TURNER,

THE LEADER

OF

THE LATE INSURRECTION

IN SOUTHAMPTON, VA.

AS FULLY AND VOLUNTARILY MADE TO

THOMAS R. GRAY,

In the prison where he was confined, and acknowledged by him to be such,
when read before the Court of Southampton: with the
certificate, under seal of the Court convened at
Jerusalem, Nov. 5, 1831, for his trial.

ALSO,

AN AUTHENTIC ACCOUNT

OF THE

WHOLE INSURRECTION,

WITH

Lists of the Whites who were Murdered,

AND OF THE

*Negroes brought before the Court of Southampton,
and there sentenced, &c.*

———

RICHMOND:

PUBLISHED BY THOMAS R. GRAY.

T. W. WHITE, PRINTER.

··········

1832.

The nation was shocked at The Confessions of
Nat Turner, *the true story of a slave rebellion in
Virginia.*

viewed Turner as a harbinger of future events—a more widespread slave rebellion that would result in much bloodshed but ultimately purge slavery from the United States. Antislavery Americans argued that such a revolt was inevitable unless the South took steps toward emancipation.

GARRISON FIGHTS ON

Garrison saw Turner's rebellion as the beginning of a slave revolution that would soon devastate the nation. An editorial in the September 3, 1831, edition of the *Liberator* stated,

> What we have so long predicted,—at the peril of being stigmatized as an alarmist and declaimer,—has commenced its fulfillment. The first step of the earthquake, which is ultimately to shake down the fabric of oppression, leaving not one stone upon another, has been made. The first drops of blood, which are but the prelude to a deluge from the gathering clouds, have fallen. The first flash of the lightning, which is to smite and consume, has been felt. The first wailings of a bereavement, which is to clothe the earth in sackcloth, have broken upon our ears.[19]

Garrison concluded that editorial with a stern warning: "Wo to this guilty land, unless she speedily repent of her evil doings! The blood of millions of her sons cries aloud for redress! IMMEDIATE EMANCIPATION can alone save her from the vengeance of Heaven, and cancel the debt of ages!"[20]

Garrison would not be intimidated by those who blamed him for Turner's rebellion. Garrison responded to the charges against him with increased and more vocal antislavery activism. In the December 29, 1832, edition of the *Liberator,* Garrison declared war on the U.S. Constitution, which he blamed for protecting slavery.

"A sacred compact, forsooth!" he wrote of the Constitution. "We pronounce it the most bloody and heaven-daring arrangement ever made by men for the continuance and protection of a system of the most atrocious villainy ever exhibited on earth." According to Garrison, the framers of the Constitution "dethroned the Most High God, and trampled beneath their feet their own solemn and heaven-attested Declaration, that all men are created equal, and endowed by their Creator with certain inalienable rights—among which are life, liberty and the pursuit of happiness."[21]

In 1833 Garrison spearheaded the movement to create the American Anti-Slavery Society, which advocated the immediate abolition of slavery in the United States.

THE AMERICAN ANTI-SLAVERY SOCIETY

The American Anti-Slavery Society was formed in 1833 at a convention in Philadelphia. A section of the declaration ratified at that convention clearly states the society's principles. It is taken from Against Slavery: An Abolitionist Reader, *edited by Mason Lowance.*

"Therefore we believe and affirm—

That there is no difference, *in principle*, between the African slave trade and American slavery;

That every American citizen, who retains a human being in involuntary bondage, is [according to Scripture] a MAN-STEALER;

That the slaves ought instantly to be set free, and brought under the protection of law;

That if they lived from the time of Pharaoh down to the present period, and had been entitled through successive generations, their right to be free could never have been alienated, but their claims would have constantly risen in solemnity;

That all those laws which are now in force, admitting the right of slavery, are therefore before God utterly null and void; being an audacious usurpation of the Divine prerogative, a daring infringement on the law of nature, a base overthrow of the very foundation of the social compact, a complete extinction of all the relations, endearments and obligations of mankind, and a presumptuous transgression of all the holy commandments—and that therefore they ought to be instantly abrogated [abolished]."

THE *AMISTAD* MUTINY

Another highly publicized slave rebellion took place aboard a ship, the *Amistad*, in 1839. The *Amistad* carried fifty-three illegally purchased slaves from Cuba to the United States. The slaves mutinied, killing two crew members and gaining control of the vessel. The slaves ordered the crew to sail for Africa, but the ship veered off course and was captured off the coast of Long Island. The slaves were imprisoned and held for trial.

The trial took place in Hartford, Connecticut. A federal judge ruled that the slaves were not legally responsible for their actions because they had been purchased illegally and were being imported into the United States in violation of the 1808 ban on slave importation. A legal appeal sent the case to the U.S. Supreme Court. John Quincy Adams, the former president, served as the slaves' attorney, and he eloquently argued that the lower court's ruling should stand. The Supreme Court concurred in Adams's argument. Mutiny charges against the *Amistad* slaves were dropped, and they were declared free men. Abolitionists cheered the outcome of the *Amistad* case.

GARRISON'S MOVEMENT GAINS MOMENTUM

During the 1830s the abolitionist movement gained momentum under Garrison's leadership. The circulation of the *Liberator* increased, and abolitionists from every sector of the United States, including the South, joined Garrison's crusade. John Greenleaf Whittier, a Massachusetts author and close friend of Garrison, attacked slavery in both poetry and prose. In 1833 Whittier published a pamphlet titled *Justice and Expediency: Or Slavery Considered with a View to Its Rightful and Effectual Remedy, Abolition*. In this document, Whittier condemned slavery as a

A drawing depicts the slave rebellion aboard the slave ship Amistad.

Garrison demands the immediate abolition of slavery in the United States at the convention of the American Anti-Slavery Society in 1840.

system of oppression that "considers rational, immortal beings as articles of traffic, vendible commodities, merchantable property." For Whittier, the only remedy for this problem was a national emancipation: "Immediate abolition of slavery; and immediate acknowledgment of the great truth, that man cannot hold property in man."[22] Whittier would later author a collection of antislavery poems titled *Voices of Freedom*, which was published in 1846.

Probably the most influential book on slavery published during the 1830s was Theodore Weld's *American Slavery As It Is: The Testimony of a Thousand Witnesses*, which appeared in 1839. Weld, who was born in Connecticut and migrated to Ohio as a young man, was a founding member of the American Anti-Slavery Society, and he published *The Bible Against Slavery* in 1837. *American Slavery As It Is* consisted largely of articles from Southern newspa-

pers, advertisements for runaway slaves, the personal narratives of slaves, and similar documents intended to depict slavery how it really was. Weld wanted to refute the proslavery argument that slavery was a benign institution that actually benefited the slaves. In the introduction to *American Slavery As It Is*, Weld asserted that "the slaves in the United States are treated with barbarous inhumanity."[23] Weld's text opened the eyes of many Americans who were indifferent to slavery by convincing them that American slavery was an inhumane institution.

ABOLITIONIST CLERGYMEN

During the 1830s many Northern clergymen joined the abolitionist crusade. In 1835 William Ellery Channing, a native of Newport, Rhode Island, and the pastor of the Federal Street Congregational Church in Boston, published the first of three abolitionist books, *Slavery*. In *Slavery*, Channing condemned slavery as an immoral institution and an offense against God:

> Our laws know no higher crime than that of reducing a man to slavery. . . .
>
> [A man] cannot be property in the sight of God and justice, because he is a Rational, Moral, Immortal Being; because created in God's image, and therefore in the highest sense his child; because created to unfold God-like faculties, and to govern himself by a Divine law written on his heart, and republished in God's word. His whole nature forbids that he should be seized as property.[24]

Channing was one of a growing number of abolitionist clergymen from New England who condemned slavery from the pulpit, asserting that enslavement was anti-Christian and violated the laws of God. Before his death in 1842, Channing would author two more abolitionist texts, *The Abolitionist*, published in 1836, and *The Duty of the Free States*, published in 1842.

Lyman Beecher (seated, center) spoke out against slavery from the pulpit while his daughter, Harriet Beecher Stowe (seated, right), would pen the most effective piece of abolitionist writing, the best-seller Uncle Tom's Cabin.

Another clergyman who used his pulpit to rail against slavery was Lyman Beecher, father of Harriet Beecher Stowe, who would, in 1852, publish the single most effective piece of abolitionist writing, the novel *Uncle Tom's Cabin*. Lyman Beecher, a New Englander by birth, migrated to Cincinnati, Ohio, in 1832 to take a faculty position at Lane Theological Seminary. With Beecher and other abolitionists on the faculty, Lane Theological Seminary became a center for abolitionist ideology in the Midwest.

AMERICAN WOMEN AGAINST SLAVERY

Men like Garrison, Channing, and Beecher spearheaded the abolitionist movement, but thousands of American women joined the abolitionist crusade. These women viewed slavery as a moral wrong that was corrupting the nation. During the nineteenth century many American women saw themselves as the keepers of the home and the guardians of the family. It was their duty to see that the family was properly clothed, fed, and sheltered in a safe home. But under slavery, thousands of human beings, children included, lived under deplorable conditions. In addition, slave families were often broken apart at the auction block when a father was sold to one master, the mother to a second master, and the children to yet another. Abolitionist women soundly condemned on moral grounds an institution that would destroy a family.

During the 1830s American women could not vote or run for public office, so they could not use the ballot box or the legislative halls to advance their political goals. They were barred from the clergy, so they could not advance their moral beliefs from the pulpit. Few women possessed the resources to establish an abolitionist newspaper as Garrison had done, but women were free to write, and many used their pens as weapons in the abolitionist crusade.

Lydia Maria Child, a Massachusetts native and the author of the widely read book *The Frugal Housewife*, a text offering practical household advice that appeared in 1829, began to write about slavery during the 1830s. Her pamphlet titled *An Appeal in Favor of That Class of Americans Called Africans* was published in 1833. Child's *Appeal* condemned slavery and urged the immediate emancipation of all American slaves. Child also advocated the removal of laws that prevented whites and blacks from marrying, a political position condemned in both the South and the North. Child was sharply criticized in the newspapers for her positions, and she was expelled from the Boston Anthenaeum, an organization for prominent Boston citizens. But Child continued her abolitionist activism undaunted. In 1841 she moved to New York City and was named the editor of the *National Anti-Slavery Standard*, the official newspaper of the American Anti-Slavery Society. That appointment made Child one of the first American women to become the editor of a major newspaper.

Angelina Grimké argued that Christianity and slavery were incompatible.

Two of the most vocal American abolitionist women during the 1830s were daughters of the South. Angelina and Sarah Grimké were born in Charleston, South Carolina, into a wealthy slaveholding family, but they developed a distaste for slavery at an early age. When they reached adulthood, both sisters migrated to New England and became practicing Quakers. Inspired by Garrison, they joined the New England abolitionist movement and began to write against slavery. In 1836 they each published influential antislavery tracts.

Sarah Grimké authored "An Epistle to the Clergy of the Southern States," an at-tack on slavery from a Christian viewpoint. She argued that God created all human beings, including slaves, in his own image and that slavery had "trampled the image of God in the dust." She criticized Southern Christians as hypocrites: "What an appalling spectacle do we now present! With one hand we clasp the cross of Christ, and with the other grasp the neck of the down-trodden slave." Sarah Grimké called slavery "the sin which the Church is fostering in her bosom."[25] She concluded her statement by urging Southern clergymen to join their Northern counterparts in the abolitionist cause.

Angelina Grimké's "An Appeal to the Christian Women of the South" urged Southern women to use their powers of moral suasion to abolish slavery in their region. She argued that Southern women could overthrow "this horrible system of oppression and cruelty, licentiousness and wrong" by appealing to their lawmakers: "Such appeals to your legislatures would be irresistible, for there is something in the heart of man which *will bend under moral suasion.*"[26] Like her sister, Angelina Grimké argued that Christianity and slavery were incompatible, that Christian women of the South had a duty to work to abolish slavery.

The Grimké sisters and Lydia Maria Child were joined by thousands of other American women who advocated the abolition of slavery. The abolitionist movement became the first significant American social movement in which women played a major role, even though they could not vote or run for public office.

The Underground Railroad

Many abolitionists, male and female, became involved in what became known as the Underground Railroad. The Underground Railroad was not literally a railroad, and it was not actually underground. It consisted of a network of abolitionists who provided safe hiding places for slaves who escaped from bondage in the South and fled toward freedom in the North.

The Underground Railroad, for the most part, operated in the slave states of the upper South—Missouri, Kentucky, Maryland, and Delaware—and in the neighboring free states—Ohio, Illinois, Pennsylvania, and New Jersey. The "conductors" on this "railroad" were dedicated abolitionists who were willing to help runaway slaves remain free. These conductors would, for example, provide refugee Kentucky slaves with transportation across the Ohio River into the free state of Ohio. Once in Ohio, the slaves would be directed to houses and hiding places where they could conceal themselves from the pursuing slave master. The escaped slaves would gradually move north, perhaps even to Canada, where slavery was illegal; assume a new identity; and live as free people.

One of the most effective conductors on the Underground Railroad was Harriet Tubman, a runaway slave. After she escaped from bondage in Maryland, Tubman returned to the South at least nineteen times over a period of several years to help her family members and others to free themselves and safely reach the free states. Historians claim that Tubman

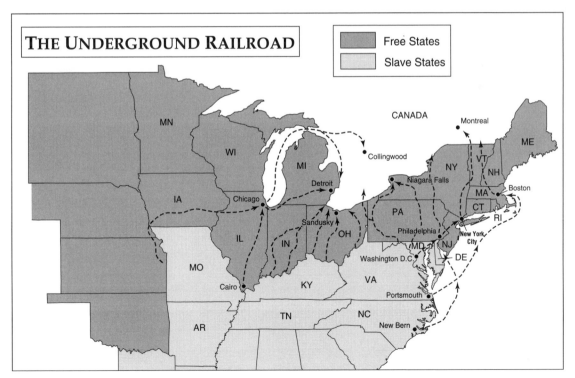

THE UNDERGROUND RAILROAD

Free States

Slave States

personally assisted hundreds of escaped slaves who eventually gained their freedom and that not one of the slaves whom she helped was ever captured and returned to slavery.

Abolitionists who assisted runaway slaves were actually breaking the law. Fugitive slave laws made it illegal to abet an escaped slave; those who helped a runaway slave could be imprisoned or fined. So anxious were Southern law enforcement officials to capture Harriet Tubman that they offered a reward of forty thousand dollars for her capture. Many aboli-

tionists who worked on the Underground Railroad were caught and convicted for the crime of helping runaway slaves, but Tubman was never apprehended.

THE SOUTHERN RESPONSE TO THE ABOLITIONIST MOVEMENT

The proponents of slavery did not stand by passively while the abolitionist movement gained force and the Underground Railroad continued to carry slaves to freedom in the North. To counter the aboli-

Harriet Tubman (standing, left) with slaves she assisted to freedom during the Civil War.

tionist message, they published proslavery newspapers, delivered fiery sermons and speeches in defense of slavery, and lobbied for stronger laws to defend slavery where it existed and to expand slavery across the American continent. They condemned the abolitionists as radicals and anarchists bent on destroying the economy and culture of the South and dividing the Union.

During the 1830s and 1840s, the proslavery argument was advanced by Southerners like George McDuffie, the governor of South Carolina. In an 1835 speech before the South Carolina legislature, McDuffie, in strident language, condemned the abolitionists as insurrectionists whose goal was to incite a slave revolution:

> Since your last adjournment, the public mind throughout the slaveholding states has been intensely, indignantly, and justly excited by the wanton, officious, and incendiary proceedings of certain societies and persons in some of the nonslaveholding states, who have been actively employed in attempting to circulate among us pamphlets, papers, and pictorial representations of the most offensive and inflammatory character, and eminently calculated to seduce our slaves from their fidelity and excite them to insurrection and massacre.[27]

In his speech McDuffie went on to call the abolitionists "wicked monsters and deluded fanatics" who had embarked on a "fiendlike errand." He suggested that "no human institution . . . is more manifestly consistent with the will of God than domestic slavery" and that the slave's "condition of servile dependence . . . is marked on the face, stamped on the skin, and evinced by the intellectual inferiority and natural improvidence of this race."[28] McDuffie argued that American slaves lived under better conditions than those of the free black people of Africa and the Irish and English working class, and that slavery preserved the South's social order. He called slavery "the cornerstone of our republican edifice."[29]

Proslavery Southerners worked politically to silence the abolitionists. In 1836, for example, Southerners in the U.S. Congress managed to enact a "gag rule" that automatically tabled any abolitionist motion or petition. Thus, congressional debate on the slavery question virtually came to an end. Southern lawmakers did not want abolitionist congressmen from the North to use the halls of Congress to advance their cause.

THE MURDER OF AN ABOLITIONIST EDITOR

On occasion the Southern antiabolitionist backlash became violent. On November 7, 1837, two hundred proslavery individuals attacked the editorial offices of the *Observer*, a weekly abolitionist newspaper published in Alton, Illinois, a town on the banks of the Mississippi River. The *Observer's* editor was Reverend Elijah Lovejoy, an abolitionist who had been driven out of St. Louis, Missouri, which is located just across the river from Alton. The attack on November 7 was not the only time

A proslavery mob vandalizes and burns the offices of abolitionist editor Reverend Elijah Lovejoy in 1837.

that the antiabolitionists had expressed their displeasure with Reverend Lovejoy and his work; three times before, antiabolitionist mobs had raided Lovejoy's offices and hurled his printing presses and other publishing equipment into the Mississippi River. But this time, the raid resulted in the loss of life.

When the angry mob surrounded the *Observer*'s office, Lovejoy, or one of his supporters, fired a gunshot from a window into the crowd. One man fell dead, and the mob attacked Lovejoy. When he held up a pistol to defend himself, Lovejoy was shot to death.

Americans on both sides of the slavery question reacted with shock to the Lovejoy incident. As in the Nat Turner insurrection several years earlier, blood had been shed over slavery. Northerners were particularly appalled by Lovejoy's death. The editor had been engaged in an activity protected by the First Amendment of the U.S. Constitution—the right to publish one's ideas without interference. Lovejoy's right to publish had been infringed on not by the federal government but by his fellow American citizens. Lovejoy's death suggested that Americans were no longer willing merely to debate the slavery issue in the press and in the legislative halls; American citizens were now willing to use violence to defend their stand on slavery.

A More Assertive Abolitionism

In the wake of Lovejoy's death, the Garrisonian abolitionists became even more strident in their condemnation of slavery, and they began to believe that their goal of uprooting American slavery would never be achieved within the nation's current political system. One of Garrison's followers, Wendell Phillips, condemned the U.S. Constitution as a proslavery document. In his treatise "The Constitution, a Pro-Slavery Compact," published in 1845, Phillips identified several specific clauses of the Constitution that revealed its proslavery character. He argued that because the Constitution accommodated slavery, "it is a 'covenant with death and an agreement with hell,' and ought to be immediately annulled. No abolitionist can consistently take office under it, or swear to support it."[30] Abolitionists who accepted Phillips's argument reasoned that supporting abolitionist candidates for public office was a waste of energy because these candidates would never be able to abolish slavery under the Constitution. Garrison and Phillips began to argue that the Northern free states should secede from the Union and establish their own Constitution that would make slavery illegal.

Not all abolitionists agreed with the extreme position of Phillips and Garrison. Hence, a rift occurred in the abolitionist movement during the late 1830s. Abolitionists who still believed that slavery could be restricted or abolished under the Constitution broke ranks with the more radical abolitionists and established the Liberty Party in 1840. The new party's goal was to promote abolitionist candidates for public office and to work to change the laws that protected slavery. In 1844 the Liberty Party ran a candidate, James Birney of Michigan, for the American presidency, though he carried only the state of New York in the November presidential election.

The Mexican War

In 1846 a series of disputes with Mexico led to the Mexican War. That conflict, which ended in 1848, resulted in the acquisition of new territories for the United States, and the acquisition of these new territories fueled the slavery debate that was already dividing the nation. Even before the war ended, David Wilmot, a member of the House of Representatives from Pennsylvania, proposed a bill that would ban slavery in any territory acquired during the war with Mexico. The Wilmot Proviso, as the bill was called, was approved by the House of Representatives, but the bill was defeated by proslavery Southerners in the Senate.

Proslavery Southerners viewed the Mexican War as an opportunity to admit additional slave states into the Union and thereby strengthen their position in the U.S. Senate and House of Representatives. They argued that Congress had no constitutional right to ban slavery in U.S. territories, that only individual states could act to ban slavery within their own jurisdictions. But antislavery Northerners claimed that

THE WILMOT PROVISO

At the start of the Mexican War, Representative David Wilmot of Pennsylvania proposed to Congress the Wilmot Proviso, which would make slavery illegal in any newly acquired U.S. territory. The Wilmot Proviso, which is excerpted here from editor Mason Lowance's Against Slavery: An Abolitionist Reader, *never received the approval of the Senate.*

"Be it further enacted, that there shall be neither slavery nor involuntary servitude in any Territory on the Continent of America, which shall hereafter be acquired by, or annexed to, the United States, except for crimes whereof the party shall have been duly convicted: Provided always, that any person escaping into such Territory, from whom labor or service is lawfully claimed, in any one of the United States, such fugitive may be lawfully reclaimed and conveyed out of said territory to the persons claiming his or her labor or service."

the Constitution gave Congress authority to rule and regulate U.S. territories. The Wilmot Proviso was reintroduced in the Senate several times, but each time it failed to gain a majority vote, leaving the question of slavery in the U.S. territories unresolved. Thus, the debate over the legality of slavery in U.S. territories would further divide the nation during the next decade.

A NEW ABOLITIONIST VOICE

As the nation was debating the issue of slavery in the territories, a fresh and articulate antislavery voice was being heard at abolitionist meetings in the Northeast. The voice belonged to Frederick Douglass, a refugee slave who was born in bondage in Maryland in 1818 and escaped

through the Underground Railroad in 1838. Shortly after gaining his freedom, Douglass spoke at one of Garrison's abolitionist rallies and impressed the audience with his oratory skills. Douglass, a self-taught reader and writer, spoke like a man with a Harvard education, and he convinced audiences of the evils of slavery by speaking honestly and passionately about his own experiences as a slave.

Garrison quickly put Douglass to work for the American Anti-Slavery Society as a speaker and writer, delivering fiery speeches on the evils of slavery and denouncing the institution in articles in the abolitionist press. In 1845 Douglass published the first of three autobiographies, *Narrative of the Life of Frederick Douglass, an American Slave.* The book, which detailed

Douglass's life of bondage, depicted the harsh and dehumanizing conditions under which most slaves lived. Douglass had witnessed women being whipped for disobeying their masters, and he had seen a slave shot to death for trying to avoid a flogging. His narrative testified to a life of grinding toil and inadequate food and clothing. Douglass poignantly described how he was separated from his mother at an early age so that neither he nor she could form close family ties; he revealed that he did not

Frederick Douglass was born into slavery and later wrote about his life.

know his own birthday; and he disclosed that he never learned the identity of his own father. In his preface to Douglass's *Narrative*, Garrison asserted that the book "contains many affecting incidents, many passages of great eloquence and power."[31]

Douglass's book was a publishing success. During its first four months of publication, five thousand copies were sold. *Narrative of the Life of Frederick Douglass* and his great speeches made Douglass famous and propelled him into a remarkable career as an orator and author. In 1847 Douglass founded his own newspaper, *North Star,* which advocated the immediate abolition of slavery and the extension of all constitutional rights to black Americans and women.

A DEEPLY DIVIDED NATION

By the late 1840s the United States had become a deeply divided nation. The antislavery agitation spearheaded by Garrison, Douglass, and other vocal abolitionists had aroused the nation to the evils of slavery. Americans who had earlier been tolerant of slavery began to view the institution with grave misgivings. Abolitionist crusaders moved from the fringes of the American political scene into the mainstream. They ran for and were elected to public office; they promoted their views in the many abolitionist papers that had commenced circulation during the 1830s and 1840s; and they advanced their views from the pulpits of churches across the North.

A Process of Dehumanization

The opening paragraph of Frederick Douglass's Narrative of the Life of Frederick Douglass, an American Slave *offers testimony to a process of dehumanization that begins when a slave is born.*

"I was born in Tuckahoe, near Hillsborough, and about twelve miles from Easton, in Talbot county, Maryland. I have no accurate knowledge of my age, never having seen any authentic record containing it. By far the larger part of the slaves know as little of their ages as horses know of theirs, and it is the wish of most masters within my knowledge to keep their slaves thus ignorant. I do not remember to have ever met a slave who could tell of his birthday. They seldom come nearer to it than planting-time, harvest-time, cherry-time, spring-time, or fall-time. A want of information concerning my own was a source of unhappiness to me even during childhood. The white children could tell their ages. I could not tell why I ought to be deprived of the same privilege. I was not allowed to make any inquiries of my master concerning it. He deemed all such inquiries on the part of a slave improper and impertinent, and evidence of a restless spirit. The nearest estimate I can give makes me now between twenty-seven and twenty-eight years of age. I come to this, from hearing my master say, some time during 1835, I was about seventeen years old."

In the face of this increased abolitionist agitation, proslavery Southerners defended their institution more strenuously. They destroyed abolitionist newspapers and pamphlets and passed laws to prevent their circulation in the South; they established what became known as a Slave Power in the federal government; and they urged their own clergymen to defend slavery on religious grounds. The nation was about to divide over slavery.

4 The Nation Divides over Slavery: 1850–1860

During the first half of the nineteenth century, the United States spread across the North American continent. The Louisiana Purchase of 1803 gave the United States a large tract of land in the middle of the continent. Texas became a part of the United States in 1845; and in 1848, after the Mexican War, Mexico ceded to the United States land that would become the Utah Territory, the New Mexico Territory, and California. Many nineteenth-century Americans believed that it was the destiny of the United States to hold all of the territory on the North American continent between Canada and Mexico; they envisioned an American republic that would unify all of the disparate territories between the Atlantic and Pacific Oceans.

Ironically, this unification process would divide rather than consolidate the nation. As new territories were acquired and the residents of those territories applied for statehood, the debate over slavery that had begun to divide the nation during the 1830s and 1840s intensified. Having failed to gain approval in the U.S. Senate, the Wilmot Proviso had not resolved the issue of whether slavery should be made legal in U.S. territories. This debate over slavery in the territories would further divide the nation and would ultimately lead to a cataclysmic civil war that would almost destroy the United States.

THE COMPROMISE OF 1850

At the end of the Mexican War, while Congress continued to debate the Wilmot Proviso, gold was discovered in California, prompting thousands of Easterners and Midwesterners to migrate to the West Coast. By September 1849 California's population had soared to one hundred thousand, and the residents applied for statehood. Early in 1850 New Mexico also applied for statehood. Both territories wanted to enter the Union as free states.

Proslavery Southerners in Congress did not wish to see two more free states added to the Union, and they attempted to block California's and New Mexico's applications for statehood. Congressmen from the free states were incensed; they demanded that the applications be evaluated on their merits and that the discussion on these applications not turn into another debate over slavery. Senators Henry Clay of Kentucky and Stephen Douglas of Illinois attempted to draft a compromise that would satisfy both parties. These two senators introduced a series of bills that became known as the Compromise of 1850.

The Compromise of 1850 had four key components: California would be admitted to the Union as a free state; Utah and New Mexico would be established as separate territories, with the question of slavery to be determined at a later date by a vote of their citizens; the selling and buying of slaves would become illegal in Washington, D.C.; and a strict fugitive slave law would be enacted to help Southern slave owners recover escaped slaves.

The extremists on both sides of the slavery debate opposed the compromise. Proslavery congressmen objected to the addition of another free state to the Union. Abolitionist lawmakers objected to the provision that would allow the citizens of the Utah and New Mexico Territories to vote to enter the Union as slave states; they argued that Congress should adopt the Wilmot Proviso, which essentially outlawed slavery in new U.S. territories. But Northern and Southern moderates gave their support to the Compromise of 1850; they believed that its adoption might settle the bitter debate between the slave and free states that was dividing the nation. The Compromise of 1850 became law in September 1850.

ABOLITIONISTS OBJECT TO THE FUGITIVE SLAVE LAW

For ardent abolitionists, the most objectionable measure of the Compromise of 1850 was the Fugitive Slave Law. This law mandated that federal commissioners would be appointed in each state to help apprehend runaway slaves. These commissioners could issue warrants, form posses, and even compel citizens in the free states to help capture fugitive slaves. An accused runaway slave who was apprehended would not have the right to a jury trial or legal counsel and could not testify in his or her own behalf. The commissioners would decide the accused individual's fate, and they would receive a fee of ten dollars for returning an accused individual to a slave owner and only five dollars for setting him or her free. Hence, the commissioners were almost certain, in most cases, to rule in favor of the slave owner.

The Fugitive Slave Law resulted in increased abolitionist agitation. Immediately after the law's passage, Theodore Parker, a Boston abolitionist clergymen, announced to his congregation that he would defy the new law:

> I am not a man who loves violence. I respect the sacredness of human life. But this I say, solemnly, that I will do all in my power to rescue any fugitive slave from the hands of any officer who attempts to return him to bondage. I will resist him as gently as I know how, but with such strength as I can command; I will ring the bells, and alarm the town; I will serve as the head, as the foot, or as hand to any body of serious and earnest men, who will go with me, with no weapons but their hands, in this

work. I will do it as readily as I would lift a man out of the water, or pluck him from the teeth of a wolf, or snatch him from the hands of a murderer.[32]

Another abolitionist, Henry David Thoreau, the writer and philosopher from Concord, Massachusetts, stated in an essay titled "Slavery in Massachusetts" that the Fugitive Slave Law "rises not to the level of the head; its natural habitat is the dirt. It was born and bred, and has its life only in the dust and mire . . . so trample it under foot."[33] In an earlier essay, "Civil Disobedience," Thoreau had articulated his wish to divorce himself from the state of Massachusetts, to live a private life without involving himself in political affairs. After the passage of the Fugitive Slave Law, however, Thoreau felt differently: "I had never respected the Government near to which I had lived, but I had foolishly thought that I might manage to live here, minding my private affairs, and forget it." But, he added, "it is not an era of repose. We have used up all our inherited freedom. If we would save our lives, we must fight for them."[34] Thereafter, Thoreau became an active speaker and writer in the abolitionist cause.

Another antislavery American who was profoundly disturbed by the passage of the new Fugitive Slave Law was Harriet

THE FUGITIVE SLAVE LAW

Abolitionists vehemently objected to section 7 of the Fugitive Slave Law of 1850, which made it illegal for any citizen to abet a runaway slave. This exerpt is found in editor Mason Lowance's Against Slavery: An Abolitionist Reader.

"SEC. 7. And be it further enacted, That any person who shall knowingly and willingly obstruct, hinder, or prevent such claimant, his agent or attorney, or any person or persons lawfully assisting him, her, or them, from arresting such a fugitive from service or labor, either with or without process aforesaid, or shall rescue or attempt to rescue such fugitive from service or labor from the custody of such claimant . . . ; or shall aid, abet, or assist such person so owing service or labor as aforesaid, directly or indirectly, to escape such claimant . . . ; or shall harbor or conceal such fugitive so as to prevent the discovery and arrest of such person . . . shall . . . be subject to a fine not exceeding one thousand dollars, and imprisonment not exceeding six months, by indictment and conviction before the District Court of the United States."

Beecher Stowe, daughter of the abolition-ist clergymen Lyman Beecher. Before 1850 Stowe had published a children's geography text and a collection of sketches and stories titled *The Mayflower; or, Sketches of Scenes and Characters Among the Descendents of the Pilgrims*. She had grown up in an abolitionist family and had married an abolitionist, Calvin Stowe, who served on the faculty with her father at Lane Theological Seminary in Ohio, but Stowe had never written about slavery. Shortly after the passage of the Fugitive Slave Law, Stowe wrote to her brother, the abolitionist minister Henry Ward Beecher, lamenting that she lacked the opportunity that he had to rail against the new law from his pulpit in Brooklyn. But Stowe's sister-in-law urged her to use the power of her pen to attack the Fugitive Slave Law. Early in 1851 Stowe wrote to Gamaliel Bailey, the editor of the *National Era*, an abolitionist newspaper, about an idea that she had for writing a series of sketches that focused on slavery. Stowe felt compelled to now write about slavery:

> Up to this year I have always felt that I had no particular call to meddle with this subject, and I dreaded to ex-pose even my own mind to the full force of its exciting power. But I feel now that the time is come when even a woman or a child who can speak a word for freedom and humanity is bound to speak. . . . I hope every woman who can write will not be silent.[35]

The June 5, 1851, edition of the *National Era* published the first two chapters of a story that Stowe titled *Uncle Tom's Cabin, or the Man That Was a Thing*. Stowe's story would develop into the most effective piece of abolitionist writing ever written.

Uncle Tom's Cabin

Uncle Tom's Cabin told the story of three fictional Kentucky slaves named Uncle Tom, Eliza Harris, and George Harris. As the story opens, Uncle Tom is sold from his kind owner, Mr. Shelby, to a slave trader who brings him southward, down the Mississippi River toward New Orleans. Eliza, hearing that Mr. Shelby has also sold her young son, Harry, escapes with the boy before the sale can be trans-acted. Eliza engineers a dramatic getaway across the Ohio River into the free state of Ohio with slave chasers on her trail. She later meets her husband, George Harris, who has also escaped from his owner via the Underground Railroad, and the Har-ris family eventually reaches the safety of Canada.

Uncle Tom does not fare as well. He is sold in New Orleans to a kind owner, but that man dies, and Tom is purchased at auction by Simon Legree, a cruel and abu-sive slave owner who works his slaves to death and then purchases replacements. Uncle Tom is eventually beaten to death at Legree's plantation for refusing to inform Legree of the whereabouts of two escaped slaves. Tom is a religious man, and on his deathbed he prays for Legree's salvation.

Stowe depicted in her story unspeak-able acts of evil perpetrated on slaves. Un-cle Tom witnesses a mother and her

Uncle Tom's Cabin by Harriet Beecher Stowe was an immediate best-seller.

children separated at a slave auction; he sees a slave commit suicide by throwing herself off a steamboat; and he hears of a slave thrown in a basement to starve to death. Stowe ended the novel with a stern warning to the nation, stating that both the North and the South "have been guilty before God" and will not avoid "that stronger law, by which injustice and cruelty shall bring on nations the wrath of Almighty God!"[36]

THE PUBLIC REACTION TO STOWE'S NOVEL

Stowe's plan for a series of sketches about Uncle Tom turned into a long novel that ran in weekly installments in the *National Era* from June 5, 1851, through April 1, 1852. Even before she had finished her final installment, she arranged for the publication of *Uncle Tom's Cabin* in book format. The novel was an immediate best-seller; it sold more than fifty thousand copies in its first six weeks on the market. Within one year, more than three hundred thousand copies were sold in the United States, and the novel was also a best-seller in England.

The novel and its characters became the subject of lectures and church sermons, and it was discussed in literary circles as well. Abolitionist politicians made references to Stowe's work in their speeches. In the South, however, *Uncle Tom's Cabin* was condemned as abolitionist propaganda. In some areas of the South, its sale was prohibited by law. To counteract Stowe's enormously popular and affecting novel, Southern proslavery novelists began in earnest to write what became known as anti–Uncle Tom novels—fictional works that depicted kind slave

---

ELIZA'S ESCAPE IN *UNCLE TOM'S CABIN*

One of the most dramatic moments of Harriet Beecher Stowe's Uncle Tom's Cabin *occurs in chapter 7, when Eliza Harris, a runaway slave, and her child escape from Kentucky to Ohio by dashing across ice floes streaming down the Ohio River.*

"A thousand lives seemed to be concentrated in that one moment to Eliza. Her room opened by a side door to the river. She caught her child, and sprang down the steps towards it. The [slave] trader caught a full glimpse of her, just as she was disappearing down the bank; and throwing himself from his horse, calling loudly on Sam and Andy, he was after her like a hound after a deer. In that dizzy moment her feet to her scarce seemed to touch the ground, and a moment brought her to the water's edge. Right behind they came; and, nerved with strength such as God gives only to the desperate, with one wild cry and flying leap, she vaulted sheer over the turbid current by the shore, on to the raft of ice beyond. It was a desperate leap—impossible to anything but madness and despair. . . .

The huge green fragment of ice on which she alighted pitched and creaked as her weight came on it, but she stayed there not a moment. With wild cries and desperate energy she leaped to another and still another cake;—stumbling—leaping—slipping—springing upwards again! Her shoes are gone—her stockings cut from her feet—while blood marked every step; but she saw nothing, felt nothing, till dimly, as in a dream, she saw the Ohio side, and a man helping her up the bank."

owners and slaves who were pleased with their situation.

Stowe's novel had succeeded in escalating the already intense national debate over slavery. When President Abraham Lincoln met Stowe at a White House reception during the Civil War, he is alleged to have said, "So you're the little woman who wrote the book that started this great war!"[37] Lincoln's statement might be a slight exaggeration, but there is no doubt that Stowe's abolitionist text further divided a nation that was already bitterly at odds over slavery.

THE KANSAS CRISIS

As Americans read and debated *Uncle Tom's Cabin*, another national crisis was looming. The Compromise of 1850 did not completely resolve the issue of whether slavery should be allowed in U.S. territories. In 1854 settlers residing in the Kansas-Nebraska Territory applied for statehood. The debate over this territory's admission to the Union triggered another bitter debate over slavery. Senator Stephen Douglas of Illinois, trying to forge a compromise that would satisfy both proslavery and antislavery congressmen, proposed that the territory be divided into two sections—Kansas and Nebraska—and that the residents of each territory be allowed to decide, at the ballot box, whether slavery should be allowed or outlawed. Douglas referred to his plan for local residents to decide on slavery as "popular sovereignty." In May 1854, after an extended and contentious debate, Congress passed Douglas's Kansas-Nebraska Act.

Abolitionists condemned Douglas's bill. They did not wish to see slavery spread into any new territories, and the bill allowed that possibility if enough proslavery Americans settled in Kansas or Nebraska. Daniel Webster, an antislavery senator from Massachusetts, supported the Kansas-Nebraska Act as a reasonable compromise, and his constituents labeled him a traitor to the abolitionist cause for supporting a bill that might extend slavery.

Kansas would be the first of the two territories to decide on the issue of slavery, and both proslavery and antislavery settlers began moving there to cast their ballots in the upcoming vote. Not long afterward, violence erupted between the two factions. The fighting spread across the territory, and Kansas became known as "Bleeding Kansas."

One of the abolitionist crusaders who entered the Kansas war was John Brown, an Ohio man who joined his sons in Kansas when they informed him that a civil war had broken out. During one night of terror, Brown and his sons brutally murdered several proslavery settlers. Federal troops eventually entered Kansas to stop the violence—after more than two hundred lives had been lost—and Brown returned to Ohio to form another plan to strike out against slavery.

THE EMERGENCE OF ABRAHAM LINCOLN

The passage of the Kansas-Nebraska Act upset many moderate Northerners who were willing to tolerate slavery in the

In 1854 the debate over slavery erupted in violence as abolitionist and proslavery factions fought for control of the Kansas Territory.

South—where it had long existed—but who opposed its spread to new territories. One of those Northerners was Abraham Lincoln of Illinois. He had served one undistinguished term in the House of Representatives during the 1840s. In 1854, when the Kansas-Nebraska Act was passed, he was temporarily retired from politics and working as an attorney in Illinois. Soon after the passage of that bill, he began to condemn it in a series of speeches delivered in Illinois cities and towns.

In a speech in Peoria, Illinois, delivered on October 16, 1854, Lincoln, who had al-ways found slavery morally troubling but who had never joined the abolitionist crusade, stated, "This *declared* indifference, but as I must think, covert *real* zeal for spread of slavery, I can not but hate. I hate it because of the monstrous injustice of slavery itself."[38] In Lincoln's view, slavery violated the spirit of the Declaration of Independence. In the passage of the Kansas-Nebraska Act and the public's acceptance of the concept of popular sovereignty, Lincoln saw the potential to spread slavery across the American continent—an alarming prospect even for those Americans who had tolerated slavery in the South.

THE *DRED SCOTT* CASE

In 1857 the U.S. Supreme Court handed down a decision that would further anger Lincoln and other Americans who did not wish to see slavery extended to new U.S. territories and states. The case involved a slave named Dred Scott.

Scott was a Missouri slave who had accompanied his master, John Emerson, to the free territory of Minnesota and the free state of Illinois. After Scott and Emerson returned to Missouri, Emerson died. At that point, Scott sued for his freedom, claiming that he had become a free man while living in free territory. Mrs. Emerson maintained that Scott remained her late husband's property even though they had resided for a time in Minnesota and Illinois. Scott lost his case in court but appealed the ruling through the federal court system. The case went all the way to the Supreme Court, where judgment on legal issues is binding on all parties. In 1857 the Supreme Court ruled against Scott; he would remain a slave.

The ruling troubled antislavery Americans. Chief Justice Roger Taney ruled that Scott, a slave, was not a citizen—he was, legally speaking, a piece of property—and, therefore, he could not appeal his case to the Supreme Court. Because Scott was a piece of property, his owner retained possession of him when he moved to a free state or territory, just as Scott's owner would retain possession of a wagon or a horse when he traveled from a slave to a free state. In addition, the High Court asserted that Congress had no legal right to outlaw slavery in any U.S. territory.

REACTION TO THE *DRED SCOTT* DECISION

Proslavery Southerners applauded the Supreme Court's decision. They had always considered slaves property, and they had always opposed any measure taken by the federal government to restrict or outlaw slavery in any region of the United States. Now the Supreme Court had validated those beliefs.

Abolitionists were terrified of the long-term implications of the *Dred Scott* decision. If Congress had no right to restrict slavery in U.S. territories, then slavery could spread unchecked across the American continent. Furthermore, if one slave owner, John Emerson, could bring one slave, Dred Scott, into a free state or territory and retain possession of that slave as a piece of property, what would prevent a slave owner from Missouri from bringing one hundred slaves into the free state of Illinois and settling there permanently? The *Dred Scott* decision suggested that slavery could be introduced to the free states by ambitious slave owners.

Abraham Lincoln immediately grasped the frightening implications of the *Dred Scott* decision. In his speeches delivered after that decision, Lincoln repeatedly warned of a second *Dred Scott* decision that would make slavery legal in every state. In Lincoln's view, not only would slavery spread to new U.S. territories, but it would also spread to states that had

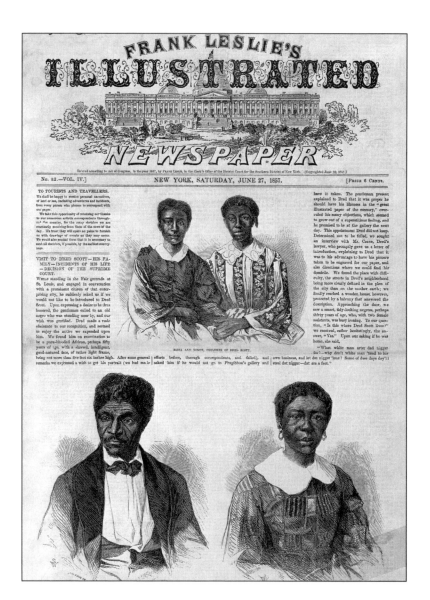

Dred Scott (bottom, left) and his family made the front page of Frank Leslie's Illustrated Newspaper *after the Supreme Court ruled against him.*

declared slavery illegal more than fifty years before.

LINCOLN RUNS FOR THE SENATE

By 1857 Lincoln had joined the Republican Party, which had formed in 1854 and dedicated itself to curtailing the spread of slavery in the United States. In 1858 the Republicans chose Lincoln to run for the U.S. Senate seat from Illinois held by Stephen Douglas. The Lincoln-Douglas campaign attracted the attention of the entire nation because the prime issue in that campaign was the issue that occupied the entire nation during the late 1850s: the extension of slavery in America. Douglas, the Democrat, championed popular sovereignty—allowing citizens of a territory or state to decide whether slavery should be legal in that state or territory. Lincoln, carrying the Republican Party banner, opposed any extension of slavery.

Lincoln kicked off his campaign with a fiery address that became known as "The House Divided" speech. Quoting the New Testament, Lincoln asserted, "A house divided against itself cannot stand." Then he applied that biblical passage to his country's current situation:

> I believe this government cannot endure, permanently half *slave* and half *free*—but I *do* believe it will cease to be divided.
>
> I do not expect the Union to be *dissolved*—I do not expect the house to *fall*—but I *do* expect it will cease to be divided.
>
> It will become *all* one thing, or *all* the other.
>
> Either the *opponents* of slavery, will arrest the further spread of it, and place it where the public mind shall rest in the belief that it is in course of ultimate extinction; or its *advocates* will push it forward, till it shall become alike lawful in *all* the States, old as well as *new*—*North* as well as *South*.
>
> Have we no *tendency* to the latter condition?[39]

In "The House Divided" speech, Lincoln reiterated the themes that he had sounded since he reentered politics in

1854: the wrong-headedness of the Kansas-Nebraska Act, the dangerous implications of the *Dred Scott* decision, and the right of the federal government to restrict slavery.

THE LINCOLN-DOUGLAS DEBATES

The Lincoln-Douglas campaign featured a series of seven debates in cities and towns around Illinois in which the two candidates spoke directly to the voters on the key issues of the day. During these debates, Lincoln articulated the Republican opposition to the spread of slavery. He challenged the morality of slavery, questioning whether the institution squared with the clauses about human rights included in the Declaration of Independence. Douglas defended popular sovereignty. Transcripts of the debates were published in newspapers around the nation, so Americans all over the country were able to follow the Lincoln-Douglas campaign and get to know the candidates and their positions. By election day, Lincoln had become the favorite candidate of antislavery Americans in the Midwest and in the Northeast.

Although Lincoln ran an energetic campaign, Douglas, the incumbent, emerged the victor in the 1858 Illinois Senate race. But Lincoln did not go quietly into retirement after his electoral defeat; he continued making speeches across the Northeast and the Midwest on the slavery issue. Despite his defeat in the Illinois Senate race, Lincoln was considering a run for the presidency in the election of 1860.

Abraham Lincoln speaks directly to the voters about the Republican Party's opposition to slavery during his campaign for the senate in 1858.

In his speeches, Lincoln stressed that the forces determined to restrict American slavery seemed to be in retreat. The Kansas-Nebraska Act and the *Dred Scott* decision suggested that the "Slave Power"—the slaveholding Southern plantation owners and the politicians who supported them—were gaining momentum in their effort to spread slavery across the United States. But he urged antislavery Americans not to give up their effort to limit the spread of slavery. In a speech delivered in Columbus, Ohio, on September 16, 1859, for example, Lincoln warned of the "great danger of the institution of slavery being spread out and extended, until it is ultimately made alike lawful in all of the States of this Union; so believing, to prevent that incidental and ultimate consummation, is the original and chief purpose of the Republican organization."[40]

JOHN BROWN'S PLOT

One abolitionist, John Brown, who had fought the proslavery forces in Kansas in 1855, was, like Lincoln, especially troubled by the Slave Power's recent advances. Brown had returned to Ohio after the Kansas civil war and had begun planning a bold move against the Slave Power.

He later traveled to Massachusetts and met William Lloyd Garrison, Theodore Parker, Henry David Thoreau, and other leaders in the abolitionist movement. Secretly, he began to recruit the men and solicit the money and weapons necessary to put his plan into effect.

Brown planned to ignite a massive slave insurrection. He would begin his work in Harpers Ferry, Virginia, where weapons for the U.S. military were produced and stored. Brown intended to take over the Harpers Ferry arsenal, arm the slaves on nearby farms and plantations, and incite them to begin a slave revolt that would spread throughout Virginia and Maryland and eventually encompass the entire South. Brown was tired of listening to abolitionist speeches and reading anti-slavery pamphlets and newspapers. He sensed that such agitation was ineffective. The abolitionist movement had been in high gear for more than two decades, and slavery seemed to be spreading across the United States. Brown wished to take swift and bold action against the Slave Power.

JOHN BROWN'S RAID

Brown arrived in Harpers Ferry in early July 1859. He rented a farmhouse outside

JOHN BROWN ADDRESSES THE COURT

Before sentencing John Brown, Judge Richard Parker asked Brown if he wished to address the court. Brown offered a religious defense for his actions, as this excerpt from his speech suggests. It is found in editor Diane Ravitch's The American Reader: Words That Moved a Nation.

"This Court acknowledges, too, as I suppose, the validity of the law of God. I see a book kissed, which I suppose to be the Bible, or at least the New Testament, which teaches me that all things whatsoever I would that men should do to me, I should do even so to them. It teaches me, further, to remember them that are in bonds as bound with them. I endeavored to act up to that instruction. I say I am yet too young to understand that God is any respecter of persons. I believe that to have interfered as I have done, as I have always freely admitted I have done, in behalf of His despised poor, I did no wrong, but right. Now, if it is deemed necessary that I should forfeit my life for the furtherance of the ends of justice, and mingle my blood further with the blood of my children and with the blood of millions in this slave country whose rights are disregarded by wicked, cruel, and unjust enactments, I say, let it be done."

of town, on the Maryland side of the Potomac River. During the late summer and early fall, Brown's small group of volunteers gathered at his headquarters to plan their strategy. By mid-October Brown and his crusaders were ready to strike.

On Sunday evening, October 16, 1859, Brown and his followers—twenty-two men in all—moved on Harpers Ferry. They cut telegraph lines as they moved into town. They surprised and quickly apprehended the sentries guarding the building that housed the weapons. They took control of the bridge that led to the town. Brown sent six of his men to a nearby farm to capture Harpers Ferry's most distinguished citizen, Lewis Washington, great-grandnephew of George Washington. Everything was going as planned.

But after midnight, Brown's marauders began to experience problems. One of Brown's men disobeyed Brown's order and fired a shot at a bridge watchman. The watchman scampered to the safety of a hotel and began informing people that trouble was happening. A train pulled into town, and the watchman told the conductor what was occurring. Brown foolishly allowed the train to leave town, and the conductor reported the events at Harpers Ferry at the next station. Someone contacted the state militia, and a battalion of soldiers marched into Harpers Ferry on Monday morning.

By Monday morning Brown and his raiders were trapped in Harpers Ferry. Local citizens took control of the bridge that was Brown's only escape route out of town. State militiamen were in town waiting for the signal to attack Brown's men, who had positioned themselves in a fire-engine house. After hearing about the drama that was unfolding in Harpers Ferry, President James Buchanan dispatched to the town a battalion of U.S. Marines, under the command of Colonel Robert E. Lee. Lee's troops arrived on Tuesday morning ready for combat.

After some attempt to negotiate with Brown, Lee ordered an attack. Several of Brown's men were killed immediately, and several managed to escape. Brown was beaten unconscious by one of Lee's troopers and was taken captive. Brown's plan for a great slave insurrection had failed. His rebellion lasted only thirty-six hours.

PUBLIC REACTION TO JOHN BROWN'S RAID

Southerners were outraged when they learned of the Harpers Ferry raid. They blamed the abolitionists for attempting to start a slave insurrection and a civil war. Brown's personal papers revealed that he had received financial support and encouragement from several prominent abolitionists, which suggested to Southerners that Brown's actions were part of some carefully orchestrated plot by the abolitionists rather than the actions of a handful of fanatics. Immediately after the raid several Southern congressmen met with President Buchanan and demanded a special congressional investigation of Brown's raid.

In an effort to incite a slave rebellion, abolitionist John Brown launched an unsuccessful raid on the military arsenal at Harpers Ferry, Virginia.

condemned Brown as an insurrectionist and a lawbreaker. But other abolitionists praised Brown for daring to move so boldly against slavery. Henry David Thoreau praised Brown as a man who moved "against the legions of Slavery, in obedience to an infinitely higher command."[42]

Brown was found guilty of treason and murder and was sentenced to death. Before he was hanged on December 2, 1859, Brown handed a short written message to one of the guards standing by the gallows. It read, "I John Brown am quite *certain* that the crimes of this *guilty, land: will* never be purged *away;* but with Blood. I had *as I now think: vainly* flattered myself that without *very much* bloodshed; it might be done."[43] Brown was predicting a war over slavery that would encompass the entire nation.

THE END OF THE ERA OF COMPROMISE

Brown's Harpers Ferry raid marked an end to the time when the lawmakers of the North and the South could work out peaceful compromises on issues involving slavery. "The day of compromise is passed,"[44] announced an editorial in the Charleston, South Carolina, *Mercury.* In the halls of Congress, representatives from both regions now openly spoke of the coming crisis that would divide the Union and plunge the nation into a civil war. The situation in Washington was so tense that lawmakers came to work armed for self-defense. In one session of the House of

They surmised that abolitionist senators like William Seward of New York and Charles Sumner of Massachusetts had backed Brown.

Some abolitionists tried to distance themselves from Brown; they labeled him a fanatic and a lunatic whose views were not in the abolitionist mainstream. William Lloyd Garrison's *Liberator* called Brown's raid "a misguided, wild, and apparently insane—effort."[41] Moderate Republicans like Abraham Lincoln

Representatives three days after Brown's death, a Mississippi congressman charged Representative Thaddeus Stevens, an abolitionist, with a Bowie knife. Tragedy was avoided only because several congressmen were able to act quickly and separate the two men.

Both Northerners and Southerners sensed that the upcoming presidential election of 1860 would be the most important in the young nation's history. The man who would succeed President Buchanan would have to try to repair the wide rift that had developed between the nation's proslavery and antislavery factions. If the new president could not find some way to bring back

the era of compromise, he might have to deal with a civil war.

THE ELECTION OF 1860

At their convention in Chicago, the Republicans nominated Abraham Lincoln for president. During the two years since his defeat in the Illinois Senate race, Lincoln had lectured across the Midwest and Northeast on the issue of slavery. These speeches convinced Republican Party leaders that he would make an outstanding presidential candidate. Lincoln was an uncompromising defender of the Republicans' position on slavery: no expansion of

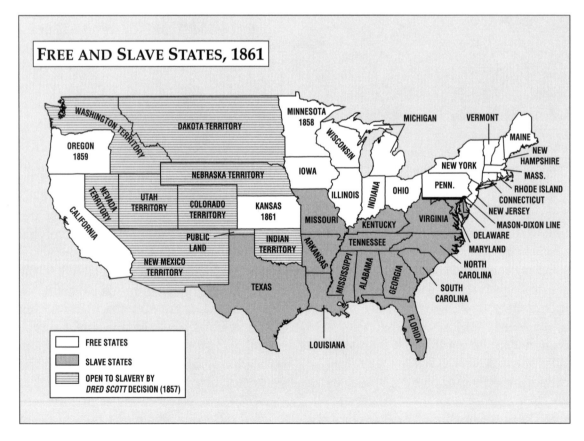

slavery in U.S. territories. But Lincoln was not an abolitionist. He realized that slavery was crucial to the economy of the South, and he believed that slavery was protected by the Constitution. Because Lincoln was a moderate on the slavery issue, Republicans sensed that he would attract the votes of the abolitionists as well as those of moderate voters.

At their convention in Charleston, South Carolina, the Democrats showed themselves to be hopelessly divided over slavery. The Democrats split into Northern and Southern factions, and each faction nominated its own presidential candidate. Northern Democrats nominated Senator Stephen Douglas of Illinois, and Southern Democrats nominated Vice President John Breckinridge. In addition, a newly formed Constitutional Union Party nominated John Bell as its candidate.

Predictably, in the November election Lincoln's opposition fragmented, and he carried the election. Lincoln won only 40 percent of the popular vote, but he carried 180 electoral votes to 72 for Breckinridge, 39 for Bell, and only 12 for Douglas. Lincoln won the electoral votes of every Northern state, but the Southern states divided their votes among Lincoln's three opponents. In March 1861 Lincoln would become the nation's sixteenth president.

THE SOUTH SECEDES FROM THE UNION

Southerners feared a Lincoln presidency. Although Lincoln had pledged not to interfere with slavery where it already existed, Southerners believed that Lincoln was really an abolitionist who would begin to take actions to uproot slavery as soon as he became president.

In December, a month after the presidential election, the South Carolina legislature voted 169 to 0 to withdraw from the United States. In January, Mississippi followed South Carolina's lead, as did Florida, Alabama, Georgia, Louisiana, and, in February, Texas. Representatives from these states met in Montgomery, Alabama, and formed the Confederate States of America, with Jefferson Davis of Mississippi as president. Most of the South was now in open rebellion against the Lincoln presidency, even though he had not yet taken office.

As Lincoln prepared for his presidency, he faced the terribly difficult task of bringing the rebellious states back into the Union without igniting a civil war. Then he would have to work with the political leaders of both the North and the South to repair the rift that had developed over slavery. He would find both tasks impossible to perform.

5 The War to End American Slavery: 1861–1864

The secession crisis that developed after Abraham Lincoln's election led to a civil war. In his inaugural address, on March 4, 1861, Lincoln tried to reach out to the rebellious Southern states that had voted to withdraw from the Union. He renewed an earlier promise not to interfere with slavery in the South: "I have no purpose, directly or indirectly, to interfere with the institution of slavery in the States where it exists. I believe I have no lawful right to do so, and I have no inclination to do so." He promised to respect the "right of each State to order and control its own domestic institutions according to its own judgment"[45] and to enforce the Fugitive Slave Law. But the rebellious Southern states would not return to the Union. The secession crisis escalated. A month after Lincoln took office, the South Carolina militia fired on federal troops occupying Fort Sumter, a garrison in Charleston Harbor. After that battle, four more Southern slave states—Virginia, North Carolina, Tennessee, and Arkansas—voted to withdraw from the Union. The North and the South were at war.

Lincoln did not wish to turn the war between North and South into a conflict over slavery. For Lincoln, the war resulted from an act of rebellion; it was an attempt by the federal government to bring the rebellious Southern states back into the Union. But the war's meaning and purpose would change during the course of four years of bloody conflict. Despite Lincoln's initial wishes, the Civil War eventually would become the war that abolished American slavery.

NOT A WAR OVER SLAVERY

In 1861 Lincoln believed that he had no constitutional right to wage a war to end American slavery. As president, he had the right to put down rebellions but not to abolish slavery. Moreover, Lincoln doubted whether the North would support a war to end slavery because most Northerners were not abolitionists. Furthermore, four slave states—Maryland, Delaware, Kentucky, and Missouri—had remained loyal to the Union. If Lincoln tried to turn the war over the Southern states' secession into a conflict over slavery, these four states might vote to secede from the Union. If Maryland voted to secede, then Washington, D.C., would be surrounded by the rebellious states of

Virginia and Maryland. The federal army might find the nation's capital impossible to defend; the capital might have to be moved to Philadelphia, New York, or some other Northern city. By forcing the federal government to move its capital, the South would score a great political victory. Foreign nations like Great Britain and France might recognize the legitimacy of the Confederate States of America; perhaps these nations might contribute to the South's war effort with money, weapons, and troops.

On July 4, 1861, Lincoln delivered a lengthy address to a special session of Congress called to deal with the war that had broken out between the North and the South. In that speech, Lincoln defined the war as a conflict over secession, not a crusade to abolish slavery: "It presents to the whole family of man, the question, whether a constitutional republic, or a democracy—a government of the people, by the same people—can, or cannot, maintain its territorial integrity, against its own domestic foes."[46] In that long address to Congress, Lincoln did not even mention slavery.

THE SOUTH'S EARLY VICTORIES

The war started badly for the North. It lost its first battle at Fort Sumter. After enduring a day and a half of bombardment, Major Robert Anderson surrendered the garrison to South Carolina's troops. The next major engagement—the Battle of Bull Run—took place shortly after Lincoln's July 4 address to Congress, and it vividly illustrated to the nation that the war ignited by the South's secession from the Union would not end quickly.

On July 16, 1861, a federal army of about thirty-five thousand troops under the command of General Irvin McDowell moved southward from Washington into Virginia. Its destination was Richmond, the capital of the Confederate States of America. Twenty-five miles from Washington, in Manassas, Virginia, McDowell's troops encountered two Confederate armies comprising about thirty-three thousand men. On July 21 the two armies clashed at Bull Run Creek. At first, McDowell's attack seemed successful, as his troops pushed the Confederates backward. But the Southerners rallied behind General Thomas Jackson, later nicknamed "Stonewall Jackson" for his determined stand against federal troops at Manassas. The Southerners drove the Yankees back, then turned their retreat into a rout as disorganized Union regiments made a hasty retreat to Washington.

McDowell's army was soundly defeated, and the number of casualties—about forty-five hundred on both sides—shocked both Northern and Southern citizens. The day after the battle Lincoln, sensing that this Southern rebellion would not be quickly suppressed, called for one hundred thousand volunteers to join the Union army to fight in this civil war.

No more major battles took place during 1861. In April 1862 General Ulysses S. Grant fought a major engagement against a Confederate army in Shiloh, Tennessee, a battle resulting in high casualties and no definite victor. The Union army's springtime military offensive along the coast of

After the defeat of federal troops at Manassas, Lincoln called for volunteers to join the Union army. These young men, the 9th Indiana Volunteers, answered the call.

Virginia—later known as the Peninsular Campaign—ended in disaster, as General Robert E. Lee's Army of Northern Virginia executed a series of brilliant military maneuvers to foil federal attacks. In August 1862 Union and Confederate armies clashed again at Manassas in a major battle that resulted in another Union defeat.

The war was not going well for the North. It had expected to crush the South's military forces quickly, take over Richmond, and force the rebellious Southern states back into the Union. But the South's determination to remain independent, not to be ruled by Lincoln's government, and the brilliant generalship of Lee prevented the North from achieving its goal. So the war dragged on.

Abolitionists Pressure Lincoln

As the war continued with no immediate end in sight, Lincoln began to receive pressure from the abolitionists in his own party to take some measure against slavery. Abolitionist leaders in Congress such as Charles Sumner of Massachusetts and Benjamin Wade of Ohio reasoned that bringing the rebellious South back into the Union with slavery in place would be senseless. Surely another conflict over slavery would arise, and the South would once again threaten to secede from the Union. Abolitionists believed that the problem of the South's secession could not be resolved unless the nation did something about slavery. In his abolitionist newspaper, Fredrick Douglass urged Lincoln to make the South pay for secession by freeing the slaves. "The Negro is the key to the situation—the pivot upon which the whole rebellion turns," he wrote. "Teach the rebels and traitors that the price they are to pay for the attempt to abolish this Government must be the abolition of slavery."[47]

But Lincoln was reluctant to take the bold step of freeing the slaves. He still doubted whether a general emancipation decree would be constitutional, and he still worried that such a decree would drive the loyal slave states from the Union. Lincoln urged the loyal slave states to free their slaves and to receive, in exchange, payments from the federal government so that those states could reimburse slave owners for their losses. However, in the summer of 1862 Lincoln was still publicly defining the war as a war to save the Union, not to abolish slavery. On August 22, 1862, he articulated that position in a letter to Horace Greeley, editor of the *New York Tribune*:

> My paramount object in this struggle *is* to save the Union, and is *not* either to save or to destroy slavery. If I could save the Union with freeing *any* slave I would do it, and if I could save it by freeing *all* the slaves I would do it; and if I could save it by freeing some and leaving others alone I would also do that. . . .
>
> I have here stated my purpose according to my view of *official* duty; and I intend no modification of my oft-expressed *personal* wish that all men every where could be free.[48]

Lincoln was not yet ready to issue an emancipation decree.

FREEDOM FOR SOME SLAVES

During the war, however, many slaves were achieving their freedom. Because much of the South's manpower enlisted in the Confederate army, plantation owners found it difficult to hire overseers to prevent the slaves from escaping. Many slaves, especially those living in states that bordered the North, found it easy to leave their plantations and escape from bondage. Thousands did escape, and many offered their services to the Union army. In the early part of the war, African Americans were prohibited from enlisting in the Union army, but many Union generals accepted the offers of escaped slaves who wished to join the Union's cause. General Ulysses S. Grant wrote in a letter to his family that he was using escaped slaves as "teamsters, hospital attendants, company cooks and so forth, thus saving soldiers to carry the musket."[49]

During the early part of the war, Congress had also acted to free some slaves. In July 1861 Congress passed a law confiscating slaves who had been forced by their masters to engage in any work that would directly aid the South's armies. In March 1862 Congress passed a measure preventing Union military personnel from returning fugitive slaves to their owners; soldiers violating this law would be subject to court-martial. In July 1862 Congress passed another slave confiscation act that freed the slaves of any owner who supported the Southern rebellion, but Lincoln disagreed with this measure and never really made an effort to enforce it.

Two Union generals, John Frémont in 1861 and David Hunter in 1862, issued orders to free the slaves in the Southern territory that their armies controlled. Lincoln revoked both generals' orders, but in his letter to General Hunter, Lincoln maintained that he himself, as commander in chief of the armed forces, had the power to free the slaves.

LINCOLN RECONSIDERS

Late in the summer of 1862 Lincoln began privately to reconsider his position on slavery. As the letters to Greeley and Hunter demonstrate, Lincoln was willing to free the slaves if it would help the Union war effort. Depriving the South of its slaves would certainly hinder its ability to wage war; upon hearing of their freedom, thousands of Southern slaves would likely leave their plantations, depriving the South of the manpower it needed to raise crops to feed its population and army. In addition, Great Britain had been considering recognizing the Confederacy. The British relied on the South's cotton for its textile mills. At the beginning of the war, Lincoln ordered a naval blockade of Southern ports, so the South's cotton could not be sent abroad. The British were considering recognizing the Confederacy and helping the South break the blockade. But Lincoln knew that the British were vehemently opposed to slavery. If the American Civil War became a war to abolish slavery, the British would be unlikely to ally themselves with the South.

By September 1862 Lincoln had decided to take the bold action of freeing the slaves. Since the beginning of the war, he had been under intense pressure from abolitionists to issue a general emancipation. He realized that freeing the slaves might impede the South's war effort. Moreover, the war was not going well for the North. With no end to the conflict in sight, Lincoln perhaps felt that the time had come for some bold and dramatic action that would energize the North by raising the stakes in the conflict. But Lincoln's cabinet members urged him to wait for a Union victory on the battlefield before issuing any emancipation proclamation. Lincoln agreed that to issue an emancipation decree while the North was losing the war would be pointless. The Battle of Antietam, fought in Maryland on September 17, 1862, provided Lincoln with an opportunity to issue an emancipation proclamation.

THE BATTLE OF ANTIETAM

In September 1862 General Lee put into action a bold plan to invade the North. Until that time, Lee had essentially fought a defensive war; he had defeated federal armies that had invaded Virginia and tried to strike at the Confederacy's capital in Richmond. But now he decided to invade the North—perhaps to take control of a Northern city like Philadelphia and force Lincoln to the peace table. On September 3 he began to march his fifty-five-thousand-man Army of Northern Virginia northward from Virginia into Maryland. A federal army of seventy-five thousand troops commanded by General George McClellan moved westward from Washington to meet Lee's army. On the morning of September 17 the two armies clashed in the farm fields along Antietam Creek near the small town of Sharpsburg, Maryland.

The Battle of Antietam comprised the single bloodiest day of fighting of the Civil War. The two armies battled from dawn through sundown, with neither side gaining any meaningful advantage. At the end of that day of fierce fighting, the Union army had incurred twelve thousand casualties, and the Army of Northern Virginia lost more than ten thousand men. After the battle, Lee withdrew his battered army from Maryland and returned to Virginia, and McClellan held his position.

Lincoln considered the Battle of Antietam a Union victory, even though it was essentially a stalemate and the Northern army incurred more casualties than Lee's force. Lincoln reasoned that the Union army had stopped Lee's advance and had forced him to retreat into Virginia. Moreover, after so many Confederate victories on the battlefield, the North had reason to celebrate a battle that resulted in a Confederate retreat. Lincoln now had a Union victory after which he could announce his plans to free the slaves.

THE EMANCIPATION PROCLAMATION

On September 22, five days after the Battle of Antietam, Lincoln issued the Preliminary Emancipation Proclamation. That document announced that, as of January 1, 1863, slaves held in the states in rebellion against the Union "shall be then, thenceforward, and forever free."[50] This proclamation was a stern warning to the rebellious Southern states that they had until January 1 to return to the Union or they would lose their slaves forever.

Predictably, the rebellious South ignored Lincoln's Preliminary Emancipation Proclamation, and abolitionists applauded it. Northern moderates, however, condemned it. They sensed that as of January 1, 1863, the war between North and South would be a war to abolish slavery. They were willing to support a war to reunite the divided country but not one to free the slaves. Northern Democrats began calling for an end to the conflict. Desertions in the Union army ran high during the last three months of 1862 because many soldiers decided that they would not fight in a war to abolish slavery. In the congressional election of November 1862, Lincoln's Republicans suffered significant losses. But Lincoln stayed his course; he refused to retract his plan to free the slaves on January 1.

The Emancipation Proclamation that Lincoln signed on January 1, 1863, did not free all American slaves; it freed the slaves only in the sections of states in rebellion against the Union that were not, on January 1, 1863, controlled by the Union army. The proclamation offered no ringing moral condemnation of slavery; it described emancipation as an "act sincerely believed to be an act of justice, warranted by the Constitution, upon military necessity" and issued by the "Commander-in-Chief of the Army and Navy of the United States in time of actual armed rebellion against authority and government of the United States, and as a fit and necessary war measure for suppressing said rebellion."[51]

Although Lincoln's document offered only a limited emancipation, abolitionists cheered its issuance. Charlotte Fortin, an African American abolitionist living in Philadelphia, wrote in her diary that January 1, 1863, was the "most glorious day

African Americans celebrate the abolition of slavery in the District of Columbia.

this nation has yet seen, I think."[52] William Lloyd Garrison, Frederick Douglass, and other abolitionist spokesmen celebrated Lincoln's decree. In their minds, Lincoln had changed the war's objective from a war to restore the Union to a war to end American slavery. The Emancipation Proclamation raised the stakes in the war. If the South lost, it could not move back into the Union with slavery intact; the South would be forced back into the Union as part of a nation forevermore free from slavery.

RECRUITING AFRICAN AMERICAN SOLDIERS

Included in the Emancipation Proclamation was a statement directed to the newly freed slaves:

And I hereby enjoin upon the people so declared to be free to abstain from all violence, unless in necessary self-defense; and I recommend to them that, in all cases when allowed, they labor faithfully for reasonable wages.

And I further declare and make known, that such persons of suitable condition, will be received into the armed service of the United States to garrison forts, positions, stations, and other places, and to man vessels of all sorts in said service.[53]

Before the issuance of the Emancipation Proclamation, African Americans had not been allowed to enlist in the U.S. armed forces, a policy that Douglass and other abolitionists sharply criticized. Now Lincoln, besides freeing the slaves, was inviting African Americans to join the Union's cause, to fight for their nation.

During the next two years, almost two hundred thousand African Americans joined the Union army and navy. With their stellar performances on the battlefield, they undermined the prejudiced views of many Northerners who believed that African Americans could not be trained or disciplined for war or that they would show themselves to be cowards on the battlefield. In a letter to an Illinois supporter who was critical of Lincoln's decision to allow African Americans to join the Union army, Lincoln described the black Union soldier as a brave warrior: "There will be some black men who can remember that, with silent tongue, and clenched teeth, and steady eye, and well-poised bayonet, they have helped mankind on to this great consumption."[54]

A WAR TO END AMERICAN SLAVERY

After January 1, 1863, the Civil War became a war fought for two purposes: to reunite the divided Union and to purge the nation of slavery. Neither of those goals could be achieved, however, unless the Union won the war. Through the early part of 1863, the South had been successful in defending itself from attacks by Lincoln's army. In the summer of 1863, however, crucial battles at Gettysburg, Pennsylvania, and Vicksburg, Mississippi, turned the tide of the war.

THE EMANCIPATION PROCLAMATION

On January 1, 1863, President Abraham Lincoln delivered the Emancipation Proclamation, which freed the slaves in the states in rebellion against the United States. The following are the key passages of that document, excerpted from Lincoln's Selected Speeches and Writings.

"And by virtue of the power, and for the purpose aforesaid, I do order and declare that all persons held as slaves within said designated States, and parts of States, are, and henceforward shall be free; and that the Executive government of the United States, including the military and naval authorities thereof, will recognize and maintain the freedom of said persons. . . .

And upon this act, sincerely believed to be an act of justice, warranted by the Constitution, upon military necessity, I invoke the considerate judgment of mankind, and the gracious favor of Almighty God."

To encourage enlistment among African Americans, the Union army took this photograph (left), to illustrate the many runaway slaves that flocked to the Union army. It was circulated with illustrations of a runaway in military uniform (right), marching into the South.

After great victories at Fredericksburg in December 1862 and at Chancellorsville in May 1863, Lee had decided to invade the North again. In June 1863 he marched his seventy-five-thousand-man Army of Northern Virginia through Maryland into Pennsylvania. Near the small town of Gettysburg, Lee's force encountered a Union army of around ninety thousand men. On the first three days of July, the two armies fought the greatest battle of the Civil War. On both sides, more than fifty thousand men were killed, wounded,

or captured during the Battle of Gettysburg, with Lee's Confederates taking the greater losses. After the battle, Lee's badly damaged army limped southward back to Virginia. At the same time that the Battle of Gettysburg was being fought, a Union army under the command of General Ulysses S. Grant was capturing the important city of Vicksburg, Mississippi, on the Mississippi River. These two great Union victories inflicted great damage on the South's major eastern and western armies, and many Southerners realized that their war for independence would eventually be lost.

THE GETTYSBURG ADDRESS

Four months after those two great Union victories, Lincoln used a speaking opportunity to state the war's new twofold purpose.

On November 19 Lincoln participated in the ceremony that dedicated a national cemetery on the Gettysburg battle site. After a long address by Edward Everett, a nationally known orator, Lincoln offered a few dedicatory remarks that became known as his Gettysburg Address. Lincoln opened his speech by redefining the war as a war fought over slavery:

"MEN OF COLOR, TO ARMS"

Since the beginning of the Civil War, Frederick Douglass had urged President Abraham Lincoln to enlist African Americans in the Union army. Lincoln's Emancipation Proclamation invited freed slaves to join the Union army and navy, and Douglass urged his fellow African Americans to act immediately upon Lincoln's invitation. The following is an excerpt from an editorial titled "Men of Color, to Arms" from Douglass's newspaper. It is reprinted in editor Richard Long's Black Writers and the American Civil War.

"When the first rebel cannon shattered the walls of Sumter and drove away its starving garrison, I predicted that the war then and there inaugurated would not be fought out entirely by white men. Every month's experience during these dreary years has confirmed that opinion. A war undertaken and brazenly carried on for the perpetual enslavement of colored men, calls logically for colored men to help suppress it. Only a moderate share of sagacity was needed to see that the arm of the slave was the best defense against the arm of the slaveholder. Hence with every reverse to the national arms, with every shout of victory raised by the slaveholding rebels, I have implored the imperiled nation to unchain against her foes, her powerful black hand. Slowly and reluctantly that appeal is beginning to be heeded. Stop not now to complain that it was not heeded sooner. It may or it may not have been best that it should not. This is not the time to discuss the question. Leave it to the future. When the war is over, the country is saved, peace is established, and the black man's rights are secured, as they will be, history with an impartial hand will dispose of that and sundry other questions. Action! Action! not criticism, is the plain duty of this hour."

Four score and seven years ago our fathers brought forth on this continent, a new nation, conceived in Liberty, and dedicated to the proposition that all men are created equal.

Now we are engaged in a great civil war, testing whether that nation, or any nation so conceived and so dedicated can long endure.[55]

Lincoln now defined the war as a war to determine whether a government established on the beliefs of America's founders in liberty for and the equality of all men would survive or collapse in disunion. Lincoln then called on members of his audience to dedicate themselves to the cause for which the soldiers at Gettysburg gave their lives, to "take increased devotion to that cause for which they gave the last full measure of devotion." He ended his 272-word address by expressing his hope that his nation "shall have a new birth of freedom—and that government of the people, by the people, for the people, shall not perish from the earth."[56]

In his Gettysburg Address, Lincoln never mentioned the words *slave* or *slavery*, but he made the point clear to his listeners that the war their countrymen were fighting was not merely a conflict over the South's secession from the Union. At stake, too, were the grand concepts of liberty and equality: freedom and equality for all Americans—concepts so clearly contradicted by the institution of slavery, which rendered some Americans as unequal to others and kept them in perpetual bondage.

Lincoln delivers his now-famous Gettysburg Address at a national cemetery dedication in 1863.

THE WAR CONTINUES

After the Union's great victories at Gettysburg and Vicksburg, the North took and held the advantage in the war, but the conflict dragged on for another twenty-

LINCOLN DEFENDS THE EMANCIPATION PROCLAMATION

Many Northerners urged President Abraham Lincoln to retract the Emancipation Proclamation. In this excerpt from a letter written to James Cook Conkling, an Illinois man who criticized the Emancipation Proclamation, Lincoln offers reasons why the proclamation cannot be retracted. This letter is found in Lincoln's Selected Speeches and Writings.

"I thought that in your struggle for the Union, to whatever extent the Negroes should cease helping the enemy, to that extent it weakened the enemy in his resistance to you. Do you think differently? I thought that whatever Negroes can be got to do as soldiers, leaves just so much less for white soldiers to do, in saving the Union. Does it appear otherwise to you? But Negroes, like other people, act upon motives. Why should they do any thing for us, if we will do nothing for them? If they stake their lives for us, they must be prompted by the strongest motive— even the promise of freedom. And the promise being made, must be kept."

one months. Union armies captured large sections of the South, defeating and pushing back Confederate armies. But the South would not be easily subdued, and the blood flowed freely on both sides.

As the war continued into its fourth year, and casualties piled up, Lincoln came under pressure to summon the South's leaders to the peace table, either to grant the South its independence or to allow it to return to the Union as it had left—with slavery in place. But Lincoln steadfastly refused to backtrack on his Emancipation Proclamation; he made it clear to the rebellious Southern states that they could not reenter the Union unless they abolished slavery. He wavered on that point only once. In August 1864, after bloody battles in Virginia and Georgia and after the Union

army had commenced a long siege of the city of Petersburg, Virginia, Lincoln, exasperated from more than three years of bitter fighting, considered dropping the abolition of slavery as a condition for reentry to the Union. However, he quickly reverted to his previously announced policy.

The war eventually wore the South down. The Confederacy could not easily replace the soldiers who were lost in combat, and the South's armies began to experience shortages in ammunition, equipment, food, and medical supplies. With the war's conclusion and a Northern victory in sight, Lincoln began to focus more closely on reestablishing the Union. But he did not plan to reconstruct the Union as it was in 1860, before the South's secession. It would be a Union free of slavery.

6 Slavery Is Abolished in America: 1864–1870

The North's victory in the Civil War meant that the era of American slavery would soon come to an end. During the final two years of the war, President Abraham Lincoln insisted that the main condition for the rebellious South's reentry to the Union would be the abolition of slavery; on that crucial point, Lincoln would not compromise. But Lincoln, a lawyer by training, realized that his Emancipation Proclamation might one day be tested in court. Would the Supreme Court, a year or two after the war ended, declare the Emancipation Proclamation unconstitutional—a violation of the Constitution's Fifth Amendment, which guarantees that a citizen cannot "be deprived of life, liberty, or property, without due process of law"? Would the Court someday rule that Lincoln, by freeing the slaves in the rebellious states, unconstitutionally deprived slave owners of their property?

During the final year of the war, Lincoln began the process of giving his emancipation decree the legal protection of a constitutional amendment. And in the aftermath of the war, Congress began a long struggle to offer full citizenship rights to the former slaves.

These efforts were designed to guarantee that in the reconstructed Union, the rights articulated in the Declaration of Independence would apply equally to all Americans regardless of race.

LINCOLN SUPPORTS ABOLITIONIST EFFORTS IN THE LOYAL SLAVE STATES

In June 1863 Lincoln supported the effort in Missouri, a slave state that did not attempt to withdraw from the Union, to rewrite its constitution to outlaw slavery. He supported a similar effort in Maryland in 1864, and he urged that Delaware and Kentucky, the remaining loyal slave states, undertake the same effort to rewrite their constitutions to prohibit slavery.

At the same time, Louisiana, which had come under Union control early in the war, and Arkansas began to draft antislavery state constitutions. Lincoln pledged his support for any rebellious state that wanted to reenter the Union after abolishing slavery within its borders. Congress was in the process of discussing more stringent conditions that the rebellious states would have to meet before rejoining the Union, but Lincoln urged each state to propose its own individual reentry plan; he would urge Congress to approve of any such plan that included an acceptance of the Emancipation Proclamation.

THE THIRTEENTH AMENDMENT

Early in 1864 Congress began discussing adding a thirteenth amendment to the Constitution that would forever outlaw slavery in the United States and its territories. Such an amendment would guarantee that no court could ever invalidate Lincoln's Emancipation Proclamation.

The process of amending the Constitution is a difficult one. First, a proposed amendment must be approved by two-thirds of the U.S. Senate and two-thirds of the House of Representatives. After obtaining approval by Congress, the proposed amendment would have to be approved by three-quarters of the individual state legislatures. The men who authored the Constitution wanted to ensure that the document would not be amended for flimsy or inadequate reasons, so these men decided that the Constitution would be amended only if an overwhelming majority of the nation's lawmakers approved of the change.

In April 1864 the proposed Thirteenth Amendment gained the approval of two-thirds of the Senate, but it failed to receive the necessary two-thirds of the votes in the House of Representatives, so the process of amending the Constitution came to a halt. But Lincoln was fully behind the measure. When he ran for reelection in 1864, he urged the Republican Party to make passage of the Thirteenth Amendment part of its campaign platform. Party leaders agreed with Lincoln, and Lincoln's convincing reelection in November guaranteed that the man who occupied the White House for the next presidential term would continue to push for passage of the Thirteenth Amendment.

Immediately after his reelection, Lincoln urged members of the House of Representatives who had voted against the Thirteenth Amendment to reconsider their votes. In his annual address to Congress, delivered on December 6, 1864, Lincoln asserted that American voters had expressed their support for the amendment in the November election. "It is the voice of the people now, for the first time, heard upon the question," stated Lincoln. "In a great national crisis, like ours, unanimity of action among those seeking a common end is very desirable—almost indispensable."[57] On January 31, 1865, members of the House of Representatives heeded Lincoln's advice and passed the Thirteenth Amendment. The new amendment was brief, comprising two one-sentence sections:

> Section 1. Neither slavery nor involuntary servitude, except as a punishment for crime whereof the party shall have been duly convicted, shall exist within the United States, or any place subject to their jurisdiction.

> Section 2. Congress shall have the power to enforce this article by appropriate legislation.

The new amendment would also have to be approved by three-quarters of the individual state legislatures before it became a permanent part of the Constitution. The legislatures of the Northern states quickly approved the proposed amendment, but the rebellious Southern states would have to be included in the three-quarters count. As a result, as the war came to an end, Lincoln and Congress insisted that rebellious states could rejoin the Union only if their legislatures voted to approve the Thirteenth Amendment.

LINCOLN'S SECOND INAUGURAL ADDRESS

On March 4, 1865, as the war was in its final weeks, Lincoln took the oath for his second presidential term. As part of a tradition dating to President George Washington, a newly sworn-in U.S. president delivered an inaugural address that presented to the American people some goals for the new administration. At his second inauguration, however, Lincoln delivered a speech very different from inaugural addresses of the past. Lincoln, the reluctant abolitionist, delivered to his countrymen a rousing sermon on the evils of slavery.

He began his inaugural address by expressing his hope that the Union army would soon finish its work. Then he looked briefly backward to his first inauguration four years earlier. At that time, he stated, he had devoted himself to "*saving* the Union without war," while "insurgent agents were in the city seeking to

---

THE SECOND INAUGURAL ADDRESS: A TRUTH NEEDED TO BE TOLD

Abraham Lincoln felt that his second inaugural address was perhaps his greatest speech. He expressed that sentiment to his friend Thurlow Weed in a letter dated March 15, 1865, and excerpted from his Selected Speeches and Writings.

"Every one likes a compliment. Thank you for yours on my little notification speech, and on the recent Inaugural Address. I expect the latter to wear as well as—perhaps better than—any thing I have produced; but I believe it is not immediately popular. Men are not flattered by being shown that there has been a difference of purpose between the Almighty and them. To deny it, however, in this case, is to deny that there is a God governing the world. It is a truth which I thought needed to be told; and as whatever humiliation there is in it, falls most directly on myself, I thought others might afford me to tell it."

Abraham Lincoln's second inaugural address was devoted to the evils of slavery. He felt it was his greatest speech.

destroy it without war," but still "the war came." Lincoln then clearly identified what he believed was the real cause of the war between the North and the South:

> One eighth of the whole population were colored slaves, not distributed generally over the Union, but localized in the Southern part of it. These slaves constituted a peculiar and powerful interest. All knew that this interest was, somehow, the cause of the war. To strengthen, perpetuate, and extend this interest was the object for which the insurgents would rend the Union, even by war; while the government claimed no right to do

more than to restrict the territorial enlargement of it.[58]

When the war between the North and the South broke out, Lincoln had tried not to turn the conflict into a war over slavery, but now he was admitting that slavery had been the real cause of the war.

Lincoln then sharply criticized his countrymen, both Northerners and Southerners, for their complicity in the sin of slavery:

> If we shall suppose that American Slavery is one of those offences which, in the providence of God, must needs come, but which having continued through His appointed

time, He now wills to remove, and that He gives to both North and South, this terrible war, as the woe due by those by whom the offence came, shall we discern therein any departure from those divine attributes which the believers in a Living God always ascribe to Him?[59]

Lincoln offered a brief prayer that the war might soon end: "Fondly do we hope—fervently do we pray—that this mighty scourge of war may speedily pass away." Then he continued his critique of a people who allowed slavery to exist in their land for almost two and a half centuries:

> Yet, if God wills that it [the war] continue, until all the wealth piled by the bond-man's two hundred and fifty years of unrequited toil shall be sunk, and until every drop of blood drawn with the lash, shall be paid by another drawn with the sword, as was said three thousand years ago, so still must be said "the judgments of the Lord, are true and righteous altogether.[60]

Lincoln was depicting God as a heavenly accountant who kept track of the debt accumulated during slavery's reign and now was determined to make the nation repay that debt with the blood of its sons on the battlefields of war.

Lincoln's second inaugural address provided further justification for his Emancipation Proclamation two years earlier. He explained to his countrymen that he had to act to abolish slavery. In Lincoln's view, as long as slave owners continued to demand from their slaves labor without pay, as long as they pushed their slaves by drawing blood with the lash, God would continue to require that the nation's blood be shed on the battlefield. After almost four years of death and carnage, Lincoln realized that he could not stop the bloodshed of war without ending the sin of slavery.

The president ended his second inaugural address with words of hope for the nation as it reconstructed itself in the wake of its devastating civil war:

> With malice toward none; with charity for all; with firmness in the right as God gives us to see the right, let us strive on to finish the work we are in; to bind up the nation's wounds; to care for him who shall have borne the battle, and for his widow, and his orphan—to do all which may achieve and cherish a just, and a lasting peace, among ourselves, and with all nations.[61]

THE DEATH OF LINCOLN

But Lincoln would not live to see slavery officially abolished in the United States. Just over a month after he delivered his second inaugural address, a few days after General Robert E. Lee had surrendered his army, which virtually ended the war, Lincoln was assassinated at Ford's Theatre in Washington. He was shot by John Wilkes Booth on Good Friday, April 14, 1865, and died the next day.

EMANCIPATION IS NOT ENOUGH

Frederick Douglass believed that the Thirteenth Amendment was only a first step in freeing the slaves. He argues, in this 1866 essay titled "Reconstruction," which has been reprinted in editor Richard A. Long's Black Writers and the American Civil War, *that the former slaves must be guaranteed the right to vote before they can cast off the legacy of slavery.*

"Slavery, like all other great systems of wrong, founded in the depths of human selfishness, and existing for ages, has not neglected its own conservation. It has steadily exerted an influence upon all around it favorable to its own continuance. And to-day it is so strong that it could exist, not only without law, but even against law. Custom, manners, morals, religion, are all on its side everywhere in the South; and when you add the ignorance and servility of the ex-slave to the intelligence and accustomed authority of the master, you have the conditions, not out of which slavery will again grow, but under which it is impossible for the Federal government to wholly destroy it, unless the Federal government be armed with despotic power, to blot out State authority, and station a Federal officer at every cross-road. This, of course, cannot be done, and ought not even if it could. The true way and the easiest way is to make our government entirely consistent with itself, and give to every loyal citizen the elective franchise,—a right and power which will be ever present, and will form a wall of fire for his protection."

As Americans mourned Lincoln's death, they wondered what was in store for the war-torn nation. Would the Thirteenth Amendment finally be approved? Would the rebellious Southern states be readmitted to the Union as promptly as Lincoln had hoped? And what would become of the freed slaves? Would they enjoy the full rights of American citizenship? Where would they work, and how would they support themselves? In the aftermath of war, Congress tried to deal with these serious questions.

THE THIRTEENTH AMENDMENT IS RATIFIED

Before dealing with any other issues, Congress had to wait for three-quarters of the state legislatures to approve the Thirteenth Ammendment. It was finally ratified on

December 18, 1865. Now American slavery was officially dead. Upon hearing the news, William Lloyd Garrison exclaimed, "My vocation, as an Abolitionist, thank God, is ended."[62]

But Frederick Douglass regarded the Thirteenth Amendment as only one step toward the liberation of black Americans. In Douglass's view, the emancipated slaves would not really be free until they enjoyed all of the rights of U.S. citizenship, such as the right to vote, the right to a fair trial, and the right to live and work without facing discrimination. Above all, Douglass campaigned for the right to vote. "We may be asked, I say, why we want it," Douglass asserted in a fiery 1865 address. "I will tell you why we want it. We want it because it is our *right*, first of all."[63] When the slavery question was finally settled, Douglass became the nation's leading activist for civil rights for black Americans.

The Fourteenth and Fifteenth Amendments

The activism of Douglass and other civil rights advocates prompted Congress to amend the Constitution twice more in the aftermath of the Civil War. In 1867 Congress passed and the states ratified the Fourteenth Amendment to the Constitution. This amendment attempted to extend

Many schools were established by the Freedman's Bureau to teach African American children to read and write.

equal citizenship rights to all Americans regardless of race, color, or religion. Section 1 of the five-section amendment contained the amendment's key clauses:

> Section 1. All persons born or naturalized in the United States, and subject to the jurisdiction thereof, are citizens of the United States and of the State wherein they reside. No State shall make or enforce any law which shall abridge the privileges or immunities of citizens of the United States; nor shall any State deprive any person of life, liberty, or property, without due process of law; nor deny to any person within its jurisdiction the equal protection of the laws.

This amendment attempted to give African Americans full rights of citizenship by making them citizens of the United States and of the states in which they resided and by giving them equal protection of the laws. Senator Charles Sumner of Massachusetts saw the Fourteenth Amendment as a broadly inclusive civil rights measure. "What can be broader?" he asked during the Senate's debate on the amendment. "Colored persons are citizens of the United States, and no State can abridge their privileges and immunities."[64]

The Fifteenth Amendment was enacted in 1870, and it attempted to extend voting rights to African American men. This amendment consisted of two sections, each a single sentence in length:

> Section 1. The right of citizens of the United States to vote shall not be denied or abridged by the United States or by any State on account of race, color, or previous condition of servitude.

> Section 2. The Congress shall have power to enforce this article by appropriate legislation.

Before his death, Lincoln had supported awarding the right to vote to intelligent blacks and to those who had served in the military during the war. Now, in 1870, the Fifteenth Amendment guaranteed that the right to vote could not be denied on account of race or color, and that even former slaves would be allowed to vote. This clause was included in the amendment because several Southern states, in the wake of the Civil War, had passed laws preventing former slaves from exercising their voting rights.

OTHER CIVIL RIGHTS LEGISLATION

In the aftermath of the Civil War, Congress passed additional measures designed to help the freed slaves become productive members of American society. Even before the Civil War ended, however, Congress, with Lincoln's approval, had established the Bureau of Refugees, Freedmen, and Abandoned Lands to deal with the overwhelming problems of slaves who had been recently set free. Most of these freed slaves knew little more than life on their plantations; they could not read or write and were trained only for agricultural work. Thousands were off their plantations and homeless; they were required to find homes and to

FEDERAL ASSISTANCE FOR THE FORMER SLAVES

On September 18, 1865, Congressman Thaddeus Stevens of Pennsylvania, an abolitionist and advocate for civil rights for the freed slaves, argued on the floor of the House of Representatives that the federal government must provide more assistance for former slaves. His speech is excerpted from Sanford Wexler's The Civil Rights Movement: An Eyewitness History.

"We have turned, or are about to turn, loose four million slaves without a hut to shelter them or a cent in their pockets. The infernal laws of slavery have prevented them from acquiring an education. . . . This Congress is bound to provide for them until they can take care of themselves. If we do not furnish them with homesteads, . . . if we leave them to the legislation of their late masters, we had better had left them in bondage."

work to support their families. During the postwar years the Freedmen's Bureau assisted these former slaves as they took their first steps toward personal and economic independence by providing them with work, food, shelter, and medical care. The bureau's most successful initiative was its educational program. It established about three thousand schools throughout the South, teaching freed slaves and their children to read, write, and compute. In time the Freedmen's Bureau also established technical institutes and colleges.

During the period known as the Reconstruction era, which began as the Civil War ended and lasted through the late 1870s, Congress also passed bills designed to protect the civil rights of African American citizens. The Civil Rights Act of 1866 granted citizenship rights to freed slaves and guaranteed all citizens, regardless of race, the right to enforce contracts, present lawsuits in court, and purchase property. The First Reconstruction Act, passed in 1867, provided additional legal protections to African American citizens. This act divided the South into military districts and mandated that federal troops would be stationed in each district to protect the lives and properties of African American citizens. The troops would remain in each state at least until the state amended its constitution to allow for African American suffrage.

JUSTICE DELAYED

Despite these congressional civil rights initiatives, very few freed slaves lived long enough to enjoy their full rights of citizenship. They were freed from slavery, but they remained shackled by the prejudices and discrimination that became a part of post–Civil War society, especially in the South, where the Fourteenth and Fifteenth Amendments were, for the most part, ignored. For Southern African Americans, slavery's legacy included a century of social and legal injustice, poverty, and second-class citizenship. Before 1865 the United States was a house divided by slavery. After 1865 the nation became a house divided by race.

7 The Legacy of Slavery

Senator Bill Bradley of New Jersey, in a speech delivered on the floor of the U.S. Senate in 1992, stated, "Slavery was our original sin, just as race remains our unresolved dilemma."[65] Before 1865 America was, to paraphrase Abraham Lincoln, a house divided by slavery. The Thirteenth Amendment to the U.S. Constitution abolished American slavery, but for at least another century America remained a country rigidly divided along racial lines. The legacy of slavery was a racially segregated society—especially in the South, where slavery had remained so long in place. The racial barriers that separated white and black Americans were erected in the aftermath of the Civil War, and those barriers did not begin to crumble until the 1950s and 1960s, when a great civil rights movement swept the United States.

THE BLACK CODES

The South had suffered greatly during the Civil War. Small towns such as Oxford, Mississippi, and large cities such as Richmond, Virginia and Atlanta, Georgia, were in ruins. Railroad lines were torn up.

Individual farms and homes were destroyed as the Union army swept across the South during the final year of the war. With slavery abolished, the South's plantation economy was in shambles. Many Southerners blamed the former slaves for this devastating situation and believed that they should be punished. Many communities in the South enacted what became known as the Black Codes—laws and ordinances designed to restrict the freedom of former slaves. Those who had left their plantations could be arrested for vagrancy and ordered to work without pay as punishment for their crime. Freed slaves were required to purchase expensive work permits before they applied for jobs. Southern states passed statutes that prevented African American citizens from voting and prohibited African American children from attending the new public schools that were being established throughout the South.

The Fourteenth and Fifteenth Amendments to the U.S. Constitution and the civil rights legislation passed by Congress after the war were designed to prevent this kind of overt discrimination against African American citizens. However, these federally enacted legal measures were essentially ignored throughout the South—and in parts of the North as well—during the decades following the Civil War. During that period, a rigidly divided society developed throughout the South. African Americans were restricted from living in certain neighborhoods, and they were prevented from applying for certain jobs and from attending public schools with white students.

THE KU KLUX KLAN AND THE JIM CROW ERA

Racial segregation in the South was implemented and maintained by force and violence. In 1866 Nathan Bedford Forrest of Tennessee, a former Confederate general, founded the Ku Klux Klan. The Klan, which was initially established as a political organization to promote the South's traditional values, soon became a terrorist paramilitary force whose main function was to intimidate African American citizens who tried to exercise their political and civil rights. Klan chapters soon sprouted throughout the South. Disguised in white hoods and gowns, Klansmen generally conducted their business at night. They forced black citizens out of town, burned their houses, and beat and even murdered African Americans.

Many moderate Southerners condemned the Klan for its violent tactics, but the South's lawmakers supported the organization's goals by passing legislation that denied the civil and political rights of African Americans. To prevent black citizens from voting, a stiff fee—called a poll tax—was imposed at the ballot box throughout the South. African Americans attempting to vote were forced to take and pass difficult literacy tests before casting their ballots. Statutes known as grandfather clauses also became widespread. These laws stipulated that a person who

The Ku Klux Klan, founded in 1866, is a terrorist organization that still exists today.

had a grandparent who served as a slave could not vote or exercise other civil rights.

Southern lawmakers also acted to deny the social privileges of African American citizens. Towns and cities passed laws that prevented blacks from lodging in certain hotels, eating in certain restaurants, and traveling in the same train cars as whites. Many hospitals refused to admit or care for black patients, even in emergency situations. These laws became know as Jim Crow laws—named for a character who frequently appeared in African American minstrel shows.

The Jim Crow laws seemed to contradict the civil rights legislation enacted in the decade after the Civil War. The spirit of the congressional plan for Reconstruction called for the creation of an integrated, nondiscriminatory society in the South, a society in which the former slaves and their descendants would soon enjoy and exercise their political rights, social privileges, and economic opportu-

nities. Many of these Jim Crow laws seemed blatantly contrary to the Fourteenth and Fifteenth Amendments. In the United States, the responsibility to determine whether a state law or local statute contradicted the Constitution falls on the Supreme Court. In 1896, however, the Supreme Court gave its stamp of approval to most Jim Crow legislation in a decision titled *Plessy v. Ferguson*.

HOMER PLESSY'S LAWSUIT

On June 7, 1892, Homer Plessy, a Louisiana man who was seven-eighths white and one-eighth black and considered a Negro under Louisiana law, boarded a train in New Orleans and took a seat in a car reserved for white travelers. A train detective arrested him. The detective acted in compliance with the Louisiana Railway Accommodations Act, a law passed in 1890 that required railway companies operating

Southern lawmakers passed many laws that violated the rights of African Americans such as one which prevented them from drinking from the same water fountains as whites.

in the state to provide separate accommodations for white and black passengers. Plessy was summoned to the Criminal District Court of New Orleans, where Judge John Ferguson imposed on him the penalty required by law. Plessy appealed his conviction to the Louisiana Supreme Court, which passed on the case but allowed Plessy to appeal his case to the U.S. Supreme Court.

The Supreme Court delivered its decision in the case titled *Plessy v. Ferguson* on May 6, 1896. By a 7 to 1 vote, the High Court upheld Plessy's conviction. The Court ruled that although the Fourteenth Amendment was designed to make both white and black citizens equal before the law, the amendment could not "have been intended to abolish distinctions based upon color, or to enforce social, as distinguished from political equality, or a commingling of the two races upon terms unsatisfactory to either."[66] The ruling noted that the Louisiana Railway Accommodations Act stipulated that the train cars for white and black passengers must be separate but equal; therefore, black passengers such as Plessy had received equal protection of the laws, as required by the Fourteenth Amendment.

Only Associate Justice John Harlan voted to overturn Plessy's conviction in the case of *Plessy v. Ferguson*. His written dissent argued that all citizens, regardless of race or social status, are equal before the law:

> The white race deems itself to be the dominant race in this country. And so it is, in prestige, in achievements, in education, in wealth and in power. . . . But in view of the Constitution, in the eye of the law, there is in this country no superior, dominant ruling class of citizens. There is no caste here. Our Constitution is color-blind, and neither knows nor tolerates classes among citizens. In respect of civil rights, all citizens are equal before the law.[67]

Harlan's dissent notwithstanding, this "separate but equal" doctrine became national policy. The law could mandate separate public facilities for white and black citizens, but those facilities must be of equal quality. Hence, the Jim Crow laws remained firmly in place; and during the years following the *Plessy v. Ferguson* decision, more Jim Crow legislation was enacted. Lawmakers throughout the South passed ordinances that racially segregated parks, golf courses, barbershops and beauty parlors, sports arenas, theaters, hotels, train depots, and other public places. Generally, however, the separate facilities established for black citizens were rarely the equal of those in place for whites. Thus, black children attended substandard schools, and black citizens were forced to use inferior public facilities.

THE GREAT BLACK MIGRATION

The imposition of Jim Crow legislation and the terrorist activities of the Ku Klux Klan made life in the South intolerable for many African Americans. They toiled at low-paying jobs, lived in substandard housing, had access to only low-quality

BROWN V. BOARD OF EDUCATION

In 1954 the U.S. Supreme Court ruled racial segregation in public schools unconstitutional. The following is a key passage from Chief Justice Earl Warren's decision.

"We conclude that in the field of public education the doctrine of 'separate but equal' has no place. Separate educational facilities are inherently unequal. Therefore, we hold that the plaintiffs and others similarly situated for whom the actions have been brought are, by reason of the segregation complained of, deprived of the equal protection of the laws guaranteed by the Fourteenth Amendment."

Thurgood Marshall (center) successfully argued the Brown v. Board of Education *case. He would later become a Supreme Court justice himself.*

medical care, and were insulted on a daily basis by policies that restricted their social activities. When African American citizens raised their voices in protest, or when they transgressed some Jim Crow ordinance, they might be subject to a stiff legal penalty or even a lynching. From the end of the Civil War through the 1930s thousands of African Americans were lynched or burned at the stake in the South without the benefit of a fair public trial.

To escape these conditions, many Southern blacks fled to the North. From the 1880s through the 1930s, several million Southern blacks migrated North—to

Chicago, New York, Pittsburgh, and other Northern cities where better jobs were available and where discrimination, though not entirely absent, was at least less overt. This movement of African Americans to the North has become known as the Great Black Migration.

The Beginnings of the Civil Rights Movement

Just as the era of slavery had as its legacy a racially segregated society, the abolitionist movement, too, had an enduring legacy—a civil rights movement that would eventually sweep across the entire nation. Like the abolitionist movement, the civil rights movement had a modest beginning and did not immediately achieve its goals.

The civil rights movement began immediately after American slavery was abolished. Many abolitionist leaders—Frederick Douglass, Congressman Thaddeus Stevens, Senator Charles Sumner—became actively involved in the effort to extend civil and political rights to African Americans in the aftermath of the Civil War. These civil rights activists spearheaded the movement to pass the Fourteenth and Fifteenth Amendments and the civil rights legislation of the Reconstruction period. Douglass emerged as the nation's most prominent African American civil rights advocate. He continued to write and speak on voting rights, on the need for educational programs for African Americans, and for an end to the segregation laws that were being enacted in the South. He held several im-portant government positions and used his offices to promote civil rights.

Douglass died in 1895, the same year that William Edward Burghardt Du Bois received a Ph.D. from Harvard University. After Douglass's death, W. E .B. Du Bois became the leading African American spokesman for civil rights. In 1903 Du Bois published *The Souls of Black Folk,* a major study of the lives of African Americans. In its opening paragraph Du Bois's book concisely introduces the reader to its subject matter: "The problem of the Twentieth Century is the problem of the color-line."[68] *The Souls of Black Folk* went on to become a classic African American literary text. In 1909 Du Bois gathered a group of civil

W. E. B. Du Bois (pictured) became the leading African American spokesperson for civil rights after the death of Frederick Douglass.

Du Bois Defends Civil Rights Activism

In an article published in 1910 in Crisis, *the journal of the NAACP, W. E. B. Du Bois defended his organization's activist posture. This excerpt from his article is found in Sanford Wexler's* The Civil Rights Movement: An Eyewitness History.

"Some good friends of the cause we represent fear agitation. They say, 'Do not agitate—do not make a noise; work.' They add, 'Agitation is destructive or at best negative—what is wanted is positive constructive work.' Such honest critics mistake the function of agitation. A toothache is agitation. Is a toothache a good thing? No. Is it therefore useless? No. It is supremely useful, for it tells the body of decay and death. Without it the body would suffer unknowingly. It would think: all is well, when lo! Danger lurks."

rights activists to form the National Association for the Advancement of Colored People (NAACP), which would become the most influential civil rights organization of the twentieth century. Du Bois became the editor of *Crisis*, the NAACP's journal, which became the printed voice of the American civil rights movement.

Slow Progress for Civil Rights

Despite the efforts of Du Bois and the NAACP, progress in the area of civil rights was slow during the first half of the twentieth century. In the South the Jim Crow society was firmly in place, protected by the *Plessy v. Ferguson* doctrine of "separate but equal." Lynchings continued despite many protests by the NAACP. In the North,

African Americans did not face the overt segregation that they faced in the South, but black Northerners still faced discrimination when they applied for jobs, sought housing, and attempted to integrate white society.

During the 1930s, however, the NAACP began working to repeal laws and policies that resulted in discrimination against African Americans in the field of education. Working for the NAACP, Thurgood Marshall, an attorney with a law degree from Howard University, won lawsuits that opened the University of Maryland School of Law and the University of Missouri School of Law to African American students. Before 1936 both schools had summarily rejected black applicants. In 1941 President Franklin Roosevelt, after hearing appeals from civil rights activists, established the Fair Employment Practices

Committee, whose mission was to prevent racial discrimination in defense plants. Before World War II, however, civil rights leaders were able to achieve only modest gains for African Americans.

WORLD WAR II: AN OPPORTUNITY FOR CHANGE

Thousands of African American soldiers, sailors, airmen, and nurses participated in World War II. One of the goals of that conflict was to defeat the racist regime of Adolf Hitler in Nazi Germany. Ironically, many African Americans who participated in that effort came home from the war to a society that was still rigidly divided along racial lines. In the war's aftermath, many white Americans also began to look with a critical eye at the racist practices in their own country, which tried to present itself as a symbol of freedom and democracy in the world.

In the years immediately following World War II, some of the racial barriers

Reverend Martin Luther King Jr. led the civil rights struggle during the 1950s and 1960s. He often found himself in Southern jails as a result of his demands for equal rights.

Frederick Douglass maintained that the abolition of slavery in the United States did not completely unshackle those who had been held in bondage. In this excerpt from a speech delivered in 1883 and excerpted from Sanford Wexler's The Civil Rights Movement: An Eyewitness History, *Douglass argues that African Americans are still affected by slavery.*

"Though we have had war, reconstruction, and abolition as a nation, we still linger in the shadow and blight of an extinct institution. Though the colored man is no longer subject to be bought and sold, he is still surrounded by an adverse sentiment which fetters all his movements. In his downward movement he meets no resistance, but his course upward is resented and resisted at every step of his progress."

---

that separated white and black Americans began to fall. In 1947 Jackie Robinson integrated major league baseball when he took the field for the Brooklyn Dodgers. During the next several years, most baseball teams integrated, and many African Americans became star players. In 1948 President Harry Truman, through executive order, ended a long-standing policy of segregation in the U.S. armed services. Before Truman's decree, the military had racially segregated servicemen by putting whites and blacks in separate regiments.

THE CIVIL RIGHTS MOVEMENT

The integration of major league baseball and the U.S. armed forces during the late 1940s foreshadowed a more widespread civil rights movement that commenced during the following decade. That move-

ment was ignited by a Supreme Court decision involving segregated public schools. In 1954 the Court, in the case of *Brown v. Board of Education of Topeka, Kansas,* ordered an end to racial segregation in public schools, asserting that segregation in public education violated the Fourteenth Amendment rights of African American schoolchildren by stamping them at an early age with a badge of inferiority. In legal terms, *Brown* reversed the ruling in the 1896 case of *Plessy v. Ferguson* and essentially put an end to the "separate but equal" doctrine in American law.

The *Brown* decision prepared the way for further desegregation efforts. In 1955 Reverend Martin Luther King Jr. spearheaded an effort in Montgomery, Alabama, to end segregated seating on the city's municipal buses. Encouraged by that great victory, King carried his campaign for an end to racial segregation throughout the South. In time, courts outlawed segregation in public parks, beaches, golf courses, and other public facilities. During the 1960s Congress, prompted by King's movement, passed legislation that ended segregation in hotels, restaurants, stores, theaters, stadiums, and other privately owned public gathering places. In 1965 the Voting Rights Act attempted to dismantle barriers that prevented African Americans from voting in the South.

Senator Bradley might have been correct when he suggested that American slavery's legacy is a racial dilemma that remains unresolved. But the abolitionist movement that gained momentum during the nineteenth century has also left a legacy—a tradition of civil rights activism that, slowly over time, has improved the circumstances of the descendants of Americans once held in bondage.

Notes

Chapter 1: Slavery Takes Root in America: 1619–1775

1. Quoted in Henry Louis Gates Jr., ed., *The Classic Slave Narratives*. New York: New American Library, 1987, p. 35.

2. Mason Lowance, *Against Slavery: An Abolitionist Reader*. New York: Penguin Books, 2000, p. xiv.

3. Quoted in Lowance, *Against Slavery*, pp. 12–13.

4. Quoted in Lowance, *Against Slavery*, p. 19.

5. Quoted in William Dudley, ed., *Slavery: Opposing Viewpoints*. San Diego: Greenhaven, 1992, p. 41.

6. Quoted in Lowance, *Against Slavery*, pp. 22–23.

7. Quoted in Emory Elliott, ed., *American Literature: A Prentice Hall Anthology*, vol. 1. Englewood Cliffs, NJ: Prentice-Hall, 1991, p. 409.

Chapter 2: Slavery in the Early American Republic: 1776–1830

8. Quoted in Philip S. Foner, ed., *The Basic Writings of Thomas Jefferson*. Garden City, NY: Halcyon House, 1950, p. 24.

9. Quoted in Catherine Drinker Bowen, *Miracle at Philadelphia: The Story of the Constitutional Convention*. New York: Book-of-the-Month Club, 1986, p. 203.

10. Quoted in Elliott, *American Literature*, p. 339.

11. Quoted in Foner, *The Basic Writings of Thomas Jefferson*, p. 160.

12. Quoted in Lowance, *Against Slavery*, p. 5.

13. Quoted in Foner, *The Basic Writings of Thomas Jefferson*, p. 767.

14. Quoted in Diane Ravitch, ed., *The American Reader: Words That Moved a Nation*. New York: HarperCollins, 1990, p. 101.

Chapter 3: The Beginnings of the Abolitionist Movement: 1831–1849

15. Quoted in Lowance, *Against Slavery*, p. 96.

16. Quoted in George M. Fredrickson, ed., *William Lloyd Garrison*. Englewood Cliffs, NJ: Prentice-Hall, 1968, p. 23.

17. Quoted in Kenneth S. Greenberg, ed., *The Confessions of Nat Turner and Related Documents*. Boston: Bedford Books, 1996, p. 50.

18. Quoted in Greenberg, *The Confessions of Nat Turner and Related Documents*, pp. 47–48.

19. Quoted in Greenberg, *The Confessions of Nat Turner and Related Documents*, p. 69.

20. Quoted in Greenberg, *The Confessions of Nat Turner and Related Documents*, pp. 71–72.

21. Quoted in Lowance, *Against Slavery*, p. 115.

22. Quoted in Lowance, *Against Slavery*, pp. 149–50.

23. Quoted in Lowance, *Against Slavery*, p. 225.

24. Quoted in Lowance, *Against Slavery*, pp. 180–81.

25. Quoted in Lowance, *Against Slavery*, pp. 203, 206.

26. Quoted in Lowance, *Against Slavery*, p. 198.

27. Quoted in Dudley, *Slavery*, pp. 65–66.

28. Quoted in Dudley, *Slavery*, p. 66.

29. Quoted in Dudley, *Slavery*, p. 70.

30. Quoted in Lowance, *Against Slavery*, p. 245.

31. Quoted in Frederick Douglass, *Narrative of the Life of Frederick Douglass, an American Slave.* Garden City, NY: Anchor Books, 1973, p. xv.

Chapter 4: The Nation Divides over Slavery: 1850–1860

32. Quoted in Lowance, *Against Slavery*, p. 277.

33. Henry David Thoreau, *Civil Disobedience and Other Essays.* New York: Dover Publications, 1993, p. 23.

34. Thoreau, *Civil Disobedience and Other Essays*, p. 29.

35. Quoted in Joan Hedrick, *Harriet Beecher Stowe: A Life.* New York: Oxford University Press, 1994, p. 208.

36. Harriet Beecher Stowe, *Uncle Tom's Cabin.* New York: Bantam Books, 1981, p. 446.

37. Quoted in Hedrick, *Harriet Beecher Stowe*, p. vii.

38. Abraham Lincoln, *Selected Speeches and Writings.* New York: Vintage Books, 1992, p. 94.

39. Lincoln, *Selected Speeches and Writings*, p. 131.

40. Lincoln, *Selected Speeches and Writings*, p. 221.

41. Quoted in James Tackach, *The Trial of John Brown: Radical Abolitionist.* San Diego: Lucent Books, 1998, p. 73.

42. Thoreau, *Civil Disobedience and Other Essays*, p. 36.

43. Quoted in Tackach, *The Trial of John Brown*, p. 87.

44. Quoted in Geoffrey C. Ward, Ric Burns, and Ken Burns, *The Civil War: An Illustrated History.* New York: Alfred A. Knopf, 1990, p. 5.

Chapter 5: The War to End American Slavery: 1861–1864

45. Lincoln, *Selected Speeches and Writings*, p. 284.

46. Lincoln, *Selected Speeches and Writings*, p. 304.

47. Quoted in Stephen B. Oates, *Abraham Lincoln: The Man Behind the Myths.* New York: Harper & Row, 1984, p. 98.

48. Lincoln, *Selected Speeches and Writings*, p. 343.

49. Quoted in James M. McPherson, *Battle Cry of Freedom: The Civil War Era.* New York: Oxford University Press, 1988, p. 502.

50. Lincoln, *Selected Speeches and Writings*, p. 345.

51. Lincoln, *Selected Speeches and Writings*, pp. 368–69.

52. Quoted in Richard A. Long, ed., *Black Writers and the American Civil War.* Secaucus, NJ: Blue and Grey, 1988, p. 172.

53. Lincoln, *Selected Speeches and Writings*, p. 369.

54. Lincoln, *Selected Speeches and Writings*, p. 393.

55. Lincoln, *Selected Speeches and Writings*, p. 405.

56. Lincoln, *Selected Speeches and Writings*, p. 405.

Chapter 6: Slavery Is Abolished in America: 1864–1870

57. Lincoln, *Selected Speeches and Writings*, p. 441.

58. Lincoln, *Selected Speeches and Writings*, p. 449.

59. Lincoln, *Selected Speeches and Writings*, p. 450.

60. Lincoln, *Selected Speeches and Writings*, p. 450.

61. Lincoln, *Selected Speeches and Writings*, p. 450.

62. Quoted in Eric Foner, *Reconstruction: America's Unfinished Revolution, 1863–1877*. New York: Harper & Row, 1988, p. 67.

63. Quoted in Long, *Black Writers and the American Civil War*, p. 337.

64. Quoted in Sanford Wexler, *The Civil Rights Movement: An Eyewitness History*. New York: Facts On File, 1993, p. 18.

Chapter 7: The Legacy of Slavery

65. Quoted in Wexler, *The Civil Rights Movement*, p. 265.

66. Quoted in Wexler, *The Civil Rights Movement*, p. 22.

67. Quoted in Ravitch, *The American Reader*, p. 190.

68. W. E. B. Du Bois, *The Souls of Black Folk*. New York: Penguin Books, 1989, p. 1.

For Further Reading

John Blassingame, *The Slave Community*. New York: Oxford University Press, 1979. A detailed study of the institution of slavery.

Martin Duberman, ed., *The Antislavery Vanguard*. Princeton, NJ: Princeton University Press, 1965. A collection of essays on the abolitionists.

John Hope Franklin, *From Slavery to Freedom: A History of African Americans*. Boston: McGraw-Hill, 2000. The eighth edition of Franklin's classic study of African American history.

Stephen B. Oates, *The Approaching Fury: Voices of the Storm, 1820–1861*. New York: HarperCollins, 1997. Using first-person narration, Oates allows thirteen key figures, including Harriet Beecher Stowe, Frederick Douglass, and Nat Turner, to recount the events of the decades preceding the Civil War.

———, *Our Fiery Trial: Abraham Lincoln, John Brown, and the Civil War Era*. Amherst: University of Massachusetts Press, 1979. A history of the pre–Civil War era that focuses on the activities of Brown and Lincoln.

Benjamin Quarles, *Black Abolitionists*. New York: Oxford University Press, 1969. A study of the leading African American abolitionists.

Leonard L. Richards, *The Slave Power: The Free North and Southern Domination, 1780–1860*. Baton Rouge: Louisiana State University Press, 2000. This text chronicles the rise of slavery and the rise of the South as a political force in the late-eighteenth and nineteenth centuries.

Dorothy Schneider, *Slavery in America: From Colonial Times to the Civil War*. New York: Facts On File, 2000. A history of slavery that includes photographs, chronologies, and eyewitness testimonies.

James B. Stewart, *Holy Warriors*. New York: Hill and Wang, 1976. A history of the abolitionist movement.

James Tackach, *The Emancipation Proclamation: Abolishing Slavery in the South*. San Diego: Lucent Books, 1999. A study of the road that Abraham Lincoln traveled to reach the decision to issue his Emancipation Proclamation.

———, *The Trial of John Brown: Radical Abolitionist*. San Diego: Lucent Books, 1998. A detailed history of Brown's Harpers Ferry insurrection.

———, *"Uncle Tom's Cabin": Indictment of Slavery*. San Diego: Lucent Books, 2000. A study of the most influential piece of abolitionist writing.

Works Consulted

Catherine Drinker Bowen, *Miracle at Philadelphia: The Story of the Constitutional Convention.* New York: Book-of-the-Month Club, 1986. This detailed history of the writing of the Constitution includes a discussion of how its framers handled the issue of slavery.

Frederick Douglass, *Narrative of the Life of Frederick Douglass, an American Slave.* Garden City, NY: Anchor Books, 1973. The story of the author's life as a slave and his escape from bondage.

W. E. B. Du Bois, *The Souls of Black Folk.* New York: Penguin Books, 1989. A study of African American life at the turn of the twentieth century.

William Dudley, ed., *Slavery: Opposing Viewpoints.* San Diego: Greenhaven Press, 1992. This collection of documents on slavery provides the arguments of both the institution's defenders and those dedicated to its abolition.

Emory Elliott, ed., *American Literature: A Prentice Hall Anthology.* Vol. 1. Englewood Cliffs, NJ: Prentice-Hall, 1991. An anthology of American literature, including texts from the fifteenth century through the Civil War.

Eric Foner, *Reconstruction: America's Unfinished Revolution, 1863–1877.* New York: Harper & Row, 1988. A detailed history of the Reconstruction era.

Philip S. Foner, ed., *The Basic Writings of Thomas Jefferson.* Garden City, NY: Halcyon House, 1950. This text includes both the first and final drafts of Jefferson's Declaration of Independence.

George M. Fredrickson, ed., *William Lloyd Garrison.* Englewood Cliffs, NJ: Prentice-Hall, 1968. A collection of Garrison's most famous speeches and writings.

Henry Louis Gates Jr., ed., *The Classic Slave Narratives.* New York: New American Library, 1987. This text comprises four classic African American slave narratives including *The Life of Olaudah Equiano.*

Henry Louis Gates Jr. and Nellie Y. McKay, eds., *The Norton Anthology of African American Literature.* New York: W.W. Norton, 1997. A complete anthology of African American writing that includes key abolitionist texts.

Kenneth S. Greenberg, ed., *The Confessions of Nat Turner and Related Documents.* Boston: Bedford Books, 1996. This text includes Turner's *Confession* and other documents relating to his rebellion, such as newspaper articles, court records, and maps.

Joan Hedrick, *Harriet Beecher Stowe: A Life.* New York: Oxford University Press, 1994. A Pulitzer Prize–winning biography of Stowe.

Abraham Lincoln, *Selected Speeches and Writings.* New York: Vintage Books,

1992. This text includes Lincoln's most important speeches and writings.

Richard A. Long, ed., *Black Writers and the American Civil War*. Secaucus, NJ: Blue and Grey, 1988. A collection of writings by African Americans during the Civil War.

Mason Lowance, *Against Slavery: An Abolitionist Reader*. New York: Penguin Books, 2000. An anthology of abolitionist writings from the early eighteenth century through the Civil War.

James M. McPherson, *Battle Cry of Freedom: The Civil War Era*. New York: Oxford University Press, 1988. This text details the period of American history from the 1850s through the Civil War.

Stephen B. Oates, *Abraham Lincoln: The Man Behind the Myths*. New York: Harper & Row, 1984. This text explains Lincoln's positions on the key issues of his day.

Diane Ravitch, ed., *The American Reader: Words That Moved a Nation*. New York: HarperCollins, 1990. This anthology includes key American texts from the colonial era through the 1980s.

Harriet Beecher Stowe, *Uncle Tom's Cabin*. New York: Bantam Books, 1981. Stowe's classic antislavery novel.

Henry David Thoreau, *Civil Disobedience and Other Essays*. New York: Dover Publications, 1993. A collection of Thoreau's most important essays.

Geoffrey C. Ward, Ric Burns, and Ken Burns, *The Civil War: An Illustrated History*. New York: Alfred A. Knopf, 1990. A detailed history of the Civil War.

Sanford Wexler, *The Civil Rights Movement: An Eyewitness History*. New York: Facts On File, 1993. An illustrated history of the civil rights movement that includes first-person testimonies.

Index

Picture Credits

About the Author

James Tackach, a professor of English at Roger Williams University in Bristol, Rhode Island, writes frequently about slavery. He is the editor of *Slave Narratives*, a collection of critical essays on American slave narratives, and the author of three books on slavery for young adult readers: *The Emancipation Proclamation: Abolishing Slavery in the South*, *The Trial of John Brown: Radical Abolitionist*, and *"Uncle Tom's Cabin": Indictment of Slavery*. Tackach lives in Narragansett, Rhode Island.